HESBAN

Series Editors

Lawrence T. Geraty
Øystein Sakala LaBianca

ANDREWS UNIVERSITY PRESS

in cooperation with the

INSTITUTE OF ARCHAEOLOGY
ANDREWS UNIVERSITY

BERRIEN SPRINGS, MICHIGAN

HISTORICAL FOUNDATIONS:

STUDIES OF LITERARY REFERENCES TO HESBAN AND VICINITY

Contributors

Arthur J. Ferch
Malcolm B. Russell
Werner K. Vyhmeister

Volume Editors
Lawrence T. Geraty
Leona G. Running

Associate Editor
Lori A. Haynes

Assistant Editor
Lorita E. Hubbard

Technical Assistants
James K. Brower
Larry W. Coyle
Cynthia Shuberg
Eric Shults

HESBAN 3

Published with the financial assistance of the
National Endowment for the Humanities
and Andrews University

A joint publication
of the
Institute of Archaeology
and
Andrews University Press
Berrien Springs, MI 49104

94 93 94 92 91 90 89   7 6 5 4 3 2 1

ISBN 0-943872-17-0
Library of Congress catalog card number 89-080164

Table of Contents

List of Figures

List of Plates

Preface

When Siegfried H. Horn decided in 1966 on the site of Tell Hesban, just southwest of Amman, Jordan for a major new archaeological expedition to be sponsored by Andrews University, he also commissioned one of his graduate students, Werner K. Vyhmeister, to do a study of all the pertinent historical references. Thus even before the first field season in 1968, the expedition had in hand the results of this study in Vyhmeister's B.D. thesis, "The History of Heshbon from the Literary Sources" (1967), later abridged for publication in *Andrews University Seminary Studies* 11 (1968), pages 113-125. The heart of the present volume is an edited version of the B.D. thesis done by Vyhmeister himself somewhat updated to about 1978.

Despite its value, this study had two major flaws. First it stopped with the Byzantine Period—though it had an appendix which collected references to the site by western travellers since 1806. Second it treated the biblical sources uncritically, virtually ignoring the scholarly debate on the historicity and historical value of biblical references to Heshbon. To remedy these lacks I commissioned two additional studies. The first study, "Hesban During the Arab Period: A.D. 635 to the Present," completed in 1978, was by Malcolm B. Russell, an Arabist teaching at that time in Andrews University's History Department. On a trip to the Middle East and Europe in the summer of 1977 he utilized all the original sources for this period that he could find, including those in Arabic, a language which, fortunately, he controls. The second study, "A Review of Critical Studies of Old Testament References to Heshbon," completed in 1981, was by Arthur J. Ferch, at that time a doctoral candidate in Andrews University's Old Testament Department. He argues for the priority of Numbers 21:21-31 over the deuteronomistic passages in Deuteronomy and Judges, concluding that they "describe an Israelite victory over Sihon during the conquest period and incorporate an Amorite poem (Num 21:27-30) in early Hebrew orthography commemorating an earlier Amorite conquest of Moab" (p. 55).

The series editors decided to bring these three studies by Vyhmeister, Russell, and Ferch together in a volume on *Historical Foundations.* Though they are dated, in general reflecting the scholarship of the last decade, they continue to have value beyond their historical importance to Andrews University's archaeological project. Rarely does an archaeological team have such a treasure trove of literary references to their site at their disposal. Part of our duty, then, is to relate our finds to the picture that emerges from contemporary literary sources. As this is done in other volumes it is hoped that the reader will appreciate the opportunity to return to the original literary sources collected and analyzed here.

Implicit in this volume are two assumptions that are not thoroughly defended: one is the early (15th century) date of the Israelite conquest of Transjordan and the other is the identity of modern Tell Hesban with biblical Heshbon, classical Esbus. Both could be vigorously defended, but even if alternate hypotheses are preferred, the studies here introduced still retain their value as a convenient collection of the pertinent literary references.

Arabists will take exception to the spelling *Hesban* instead of the classical *Husban* or preferred contemporary transliteration *Hisban.* In these studies *Hesban* is retained for consistency's sake because it was the transliteration used in our preliminary reports through the 1960s and 1970s, at that time employed because it was commonly used in the last century and well into the 20th century by both travellers and scholars. If we had it to do over again we would probably use *Hisban.* The biblical transliteration, *Heshbon,* is certainly the former name's linguistic equivalent whether or not these names all refer to one and the same archaeological site, which I tend to think they do—but that argument must be postponed to another volume.

Lawrence T. Geraty
South Lancaster, Massachusetts
August 8, 1988

Chapter One

THE HISTORY OF HESHBON
FROM THE LITERARY SOURCES

Werner K. Vyhmeister

Chapter One

The History of Heshbon
From the Literary Sources

The Geographical Setting

Heshbon: A City of the Central Belqa

Heshbon, modern *Ḥesbân* (Hesban), is located in Transjordan, in the region today called *el-Belqā* (Belqa).[1] The Belqa extends from the Jabbok River (*Nahr el-Zerqa*) to the River Arnon (*Wādī el-Môjib*) (Wadi el-Mojib; Abel 1933: 383, n. 1).[2] Its northern part corresponds to the (southern) "half Gilead" or "the rest of Gilead" of Deut 3:12, 13; Josh 12:2, 5; and 13:31 (Simons 1959: 36-38, 125-127; Smith 1902: 548-549). Heshbon is almost in the very center of the Belqa.

The Belqa is about 80 km long and 30 km wide, from the desert to the Jordan River (see Nichol 1954a: 374). Except for some points, all of its flat part is covered by limestone that is visible as far south as the district of Kerak (Abel 1933: 90).

Looking at the central Belqa from east to west, three clearly defined sections can be distinguished. The first one is the plateau, with an average altitude of 700 m to 800 m above sea level, and about 1,150 m above the Dead Sea (Abel 1933: 90). *Mîšôr* (Mishor, "flat country," "plain country," "plain") is the name that Deut 3:10 seems to apply to "the whole of the transjordan table-land south of Gilead" (Simons 1959: 63). Its northern end was located somewhere between Heshbon and *Mâdebā* (Madaba).[3]

Immediately to the west, bordering the tableland, the "mountains of Abarim" are found (Num 33:47, 48; Deut 32:39). The name *'Ăbārîm* (Abarim) "refers to the ridge separating the southern Transjordan tableland from the Jordan Valley, and overlooking the *Dead Sea*" (Simons 1959: 261). The ridge apparently was thought to extend as far south as the end of the Dead Sea.[4] To it belonged Mt. Nebo, identified sometimes with the Abarim.[5] This ridge is really the western edge of the plateau, cut by deep wadis that alternate with high ridges.

The Abarim fall abruptly towards the Ghor and the Dead Sea. Here we find the third section. It is called *'Arbôt Môāb* ("plains of Moab") (Num 22:1; 33:48; 36:13),[6] and refers to the plain that extends from the Jordan River to the foot of the Abarim, and from the *Wâdī Nimrîn* (W. Nimrin) to the Dead Sea (Abel 1933: 281).[7]

Several wadis cut their way down from the plateau, through the Abarim, to the "plains of Moab" and the Dead Sea. The most important ones, from the Jabbok to the Arnon, are *W. Nimrin, W. Kefrein,* and *W. Zerqā Ma'în* (W. Zerqa Ma'in).

In the vicinity of Heshbon the beginnings of several wadis are found (fig. 1.1).[8] One of these is W. Hesban, which receives the water of several smaller wadis. Its main source is *'Ain Ḥesbân* (Thomson 1885: 666). This spring is located more than 4 km from the ruins of Heshbon, "more than 100 meters lower" (Heidet 1903: col. 660). Its water is "beautifully clear . . . flowing out from a small cave under the cliff on the north side of wady Hesbân" (Thomson 1885: 666).

As W. Hesban flows through the highland, a number of pools are formed in it. After visiting the place, W. M. Thomson reported that in those little pools "there were many small fishes" (1885: 667).[9] As it enters the Jordan valley it is known as *W. Râmeh*.[10] About 5 km before reaching the Jordan River it flows into W. Kefrein (Van Zyl 1960: 50; Glueck 1951: 366). S. Merrill, who visited the place on April 10, 1876, explains that the W. Hesban is a large stream that either has to be crossed on horseback or waded (1881: 231). He also mentions that he collected in the vicinity "a good many fossils, which abound in the limestone rock in the region" (1881: 240).

One interesting geographical feature in the southwestern Belqa is the thermal waters of Callirrhoe, on the northern bank of the W. Zerqa Ma'in a few miles before it empties into the Dead Sea. They are mentioned by Pliny (*Nat. Hist.* 5.15), Josephus (*Ant.* 17.6.5), and the Madaba map (Avi-Yonah 1954: pl. 2). According to Pliny, the name "Callirrhoë itself proclaims the celebrity of its waters." This was not the only, but perhaps the most famous, of the thermal waters in the region.[11]

Location of Heshbon

The ruins of Heshbon are located at 31° 48' latitude north and 35° 48' longitude east (Conder n.d.: 267). They are mainly on two hills 893 m and 900 m above sea level (Cheyne and Black 1901: col. 2,044).[12] They rise about 60 m above the plain that starts at their base and stretch for about 550 m from the northeast to the

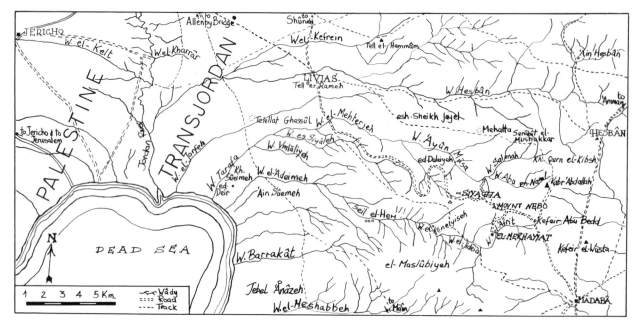

Fig 1.1   Wadis in the vicinity of Heshbon (after Saller and Bagatti 1949)

southwest. Two small valleys originate under these hills. They unite at their southwestern end and run north for about 4 km to meet W. Hesban. These two valleys formed something like a natural moat that encompassed all the city, except on the southeastern side (Heidet 1903: col. 659).

"From Heshbon a good view is obtained to the south over the great Belka plateau, and from the high top west of the ruins the Jordan valley becomes visible, with the mountains beyond . . ." (Conder 1882: 8). Merrill adds that from Heshbon the "mountains of Nebo, the ruins of Madeba, M'ain [sic], Zîza, El 'Al and other places, are in sight" (1881: 241).

Hesban today is on the western side of the modern road that runs south from 'Ammân (Amman) to Madaba, Dhîbân (Dibon), and beyond. Hesban is:

    50 km south of Nahr el-Zerqa
    45 km north of Wadi el-Mojib
    40 km north of Dibon
    30 km (20 Roman miles) east of the Jordan
      River
    22 km southwest of Amman
    14 km northeast of Ma'in
    12 km north of Madaba
    2-3 km southwest of el-'Âl

(Heidet 1903: cols. 657-663; Glueck 1934a: 6; Dajani 1966).[13]

Heshbon's Name Through the Centuries

In this section different spellings that the name Heshbon has had through the centuries will be presented in chronological sequence.

In the Hebrew OT the name appears 38 times, always spelled as חשבון. Its meaning is: device, invention (Brown, Driver, and Briggs 1907: 363-364), and account (Koehler and Baumgartner 1958: 340).

The LXX translators transliterated the name as Ἐσεβών in the canonical books (Brooke, McLean, and Thackeray 1906-1935).[14] In Judg 5:15 the expression παντας τους Εσεβωνιτας is found, with the variant τους εσεβων in the Sinaiticus and Alexandrinus codices (Rahlfs 1949). It is evidently used here as a gentilic.

Many authors[15] have considered that Χασφω[16] of 1 Macc 5:26 is a variant of Heshbon. But this opinion "has been generally abandoned" (Heidet 1903: col. 657).

Philo (ca. 20 B.C.-ca. A.D. 42) explains that Ἐσεβών means "reasonings" and "'reasonings' are riddles full of obscurity."[17]

Pliny (23-79) mentions the "Esbonitarum" Arabs (Nat. Hist. 5.12).

Josephus (37-96) used the name Ἐσεβών (Ant. 13.15.4). But he also speaks of the region or district of Ἐσεβωνιτιν (JW 2.18.1),[18] Ἐσεβωνιτιδι (JW 3.3.3), and Ἐσσεβωνιτιδος (Ant. 12.4.11).[19]

Claudius Ptolemy (2nd century A.D.), in his Geography 5.17, writes the name as Ἐσβουτα.[20]

Bronze coins of Esbus, probably all of them of the time of Elagabalus (218-222), show that the city was then called Aurelia Esbus (Hill 1922: xxxiii, pl. 5; James 1954: 1063; Avi-Yonah 1977: 117).[21] The name appears in its Greek form in the reverse of six coins, of the British Museum's collection, in the following ways: (1) AV . . . (left), ᴼVC (right) (Hill 1922: 29, pl. 5.1); (2) AVPE (left) . . . (right) (Hill 1922: 29); (3) AV (above)

[E]CB°V[C] (below) (Hill 1922: 29, pl. 5.2); (4) [AV] (above) ECB°VC (below) (Hill 1922: 29); (5) AV (above) ... (below) (Hill 1922: 30); (6) ABPECB (left) °VC (right) (Hill 1922: 30, pl. 5.3).

In two Roman milestones of the Heshbon-Livias-Jericho road built in A.D. 129 or 130 (Avi-Yonah 1977: 183-184; Thomsen 1917: 67-68), the name appears as ('αρο) 'Εσβουντος (in inscriptions of A.D. 364-375, 219?, and 236),[22] and Esb(unte) (in an inscription dated A.D. 288)[23] (Thomsen 1917: 68).

Gennadius of Esbus appears twice in the lists of bishops who attended the first ecumenical council at Nicaea (325). His name is given once as Gennadius Jabrudorum Ybutensis (Mansi 1960a: col. 694), and then as Gennadius Bunnorum (Mansi 1960a: col. 699).[24] It is rather difficult to recognize the original name of the town in these two different Latin renderings.

Eusebius (ca. 266-ca. 340) in his Librum II Chronicorum, uses the spelling 'Εσσεβων (PG 1857: cols. 407-408). Jerome (ca. 340-420), in translating his work, writes Hesebon (PL 1866: cols. 317-318). In Eusebius' Onomasticon (1966) the name is used eleven times. With its Latin transliteration, done also by Jerome, the name appears in the following forms:

Page	Greek	Latin	Page
12	'Εσβουν[25]	Esbun[26]	13
18	'Εσβουν[27]	Esbun	17
46	'Εσβους[28]	Esbus	47
76	'Εσβους[29]	Esbus	77
84	'Εσσεβων called now 'Εσβους	Esebon called now Esbus	85
104	'Εσσεβων	Esebon	10
128	'Εσσεβων[30]	Esebon	129
132	'Εσβους	Esbus	133
136	'Εσβους	Esbus	137

In his Vulgate, Jerome uses the spelling Esebon.[31]

Egeria (Aetheria), the Christian pilgrim who visited Transjordan ca. A.D. 400, claims to have seen from a distance "Hesebon ... which today is called Exebon" (1970: 69)[32]

Among the bishops at the Council of Ephesus (431) was Ζωσυς 'Εσβουντος.[33] Apparently the same bishop is mentioned in the acts of the Council of Chalcedon (451), as Ζωσιου πολεως 'Εσβουντων.[34]

In the Notitia Antiochena (ca. A.D. 570), the name appears as Essmos (PL 1855: col. 1067).[35]

A stone capital found at Râs es-Siâghah is decorated with crosses. One of these crosses has letters attached to the extremities of its arms. These letters, read in a certain order, form the name ΕΓΒΥ [Εσβου] (Saller 1941a: 265-266) (pl. 1.1).[36] The capital was found in 1933 at the east end of the north aisle of the basilica built there originally in the 5th century A.D. This basilica was destroyed in the last quarter of the 6th century, probably by an earthquake, and rebuilt completely by 597 (Saller 1941a: 45-46, 265-266).

Plate 1.1 Stone capital (bottom) with letters ECBY found at Râs es-Siâgah (after Saller 1941b)

De Vaux mentions that Georges of Cyprus (ca. 605) refers to this town as 'Εσβους (1938: 249, 254).[37]

Isidore of Seville, Spain (ca. 560-636), in his Etymologiarum 7.7.55, explains that "HESEBON" means "cogitatio, sive vinculum moeroris" (PL 1850: col. 278).

The mosaic of Ma'in (discovered between 1934 and 1937) has the name EC [BOVC] among the names and representations of several Palestinian churches. It has been dated from the last fourth of the 6th to the first half of the 7th century A.D. It was restored in A.D. 719/720 (de Vaux 1938: 227-258; Alt 1942: 68).

Pope Martin I wrote a letter in A.D. 649 to Theodoro episcopo Esbuntiorum.[38] In his letter to John of Philadelphia, written at the same time, the pope mentions again Theodorum Esbuntiorum (Mansi 1960d: col. 814).[39]

The name is next found in Tabari's (839-923) work, applied to Gabal Hesbân (Steppat 1967; Bowling 1967).[40] This same Arabic spelling (transliterated as Hesbân) appears later in The Life of Saladin, by the 12th-century writer Behâ ed-Din (1897: 97);[41] in the writings of the 14th-century Jewish traveller, Esthori b. Mose ha-Parchi (Heidet 1903: col. 658; and Tobler 1867: 33);[42] and in the writings of Ismaîl Ben Ali Abu el-Fida (ca. 1321), emir of Hamah, in Syria,[43] Dimišqi (died 1327), Qalqašandi and others (Steppat 1967).

In Marino Sanuto's map of the Holy Land (early 4th century) the name is written as *eſebon* (Sanuto 1896).

The name also appears in the 15th century in a list of bishops and other Latin ecclesiastical dignitaries of the Roman Catholic world. It is spelled as "*Esien, seu Esben*" (Eubel *et al.* 1914: 151, 286), and in parentheses *Hesebon* also is given.

The name reappears in the 19th century in the reports of travellers who visited the ruins of the old city.[44] It is the same name that we found there in the late Middle Ages, and is still the same today. Its Arabic spelling is variously transliterated as *Hesbân, Husbân, Hisbân*, etc.

Heshbon in Old Testament Times

Earliest Biblical References

Taking the biblical text as it is known today, Heshbon appears for the first time in Num 21 and in the somewhat parallel passages of Deut 1, 2, 3, and 29, as the "city of Sihon," captured by the Israelites during the fortieth year of the Exodus.

However, since the latter part of the 19th century, when historical-literary critics of the Bible rejected the Mosaic authorship of the Pentateuch, divergent views have emerged on the historicity of the event, and on the time when the documents (that, presumably, served as sources for the present biblical versions of it) were written. For a presentation of the different views developed by means of the literary-critical method, see Chapter Three.

The historicity of the Exodus is generally accepted. The presence of an Amorite king north of the Arnon cannot be considered any longer as an historical impossibility. There is no coercive evidence that Sihon did not reign in Heshbon and that Heshbon was not taken by the Israelites as they were approaching the promised land. So, for the time being at least, it seems preferable to take the biblical text in what appears to be its obvious historical sense.[45] In so doing (and based on Judg 11:26, and 1 Kgs 6:1) this chapter will also assume a 15th-century date for the Exodus.[46]

Heshbon Before the Israelite Conquest

The region where Heshbon stood is mentioned in the Bible already in Gen 14:5. Chedorlaomer and his confederates appear there as smiting successively the Rephaim in Ashteroth Karnaim,[47] the Zuzim in Ham, and the Emim in Shaveh Kirjiathaim (*i.e.*, the plain of Kirjiathaim). Kirjiathaim has been identified with *el-Qereiyât*, about 8 km northwest of Dibon (Horn 1960: 628; Abel 1933: 327). It appears in Num 32:37 as one of the cities rebuilt by the children of Reuben, together with Heshbon (*cf.* Josh 13:15-19). So the Emim are mentioned as living in that region in the 19th century B.C. These Emim were part of the race known in the

OT by the general name of *Rephaim*. At the time of the Exodus the Moabites, who had occupied part of their territory, called them *Emim* (Deut 2:10, 11). The Amorites called them *Zamzummim* (Deut 2:20, 21). At the time of the Exodus also, Og, king of Bashan, is mentioned as the only one who "remained of the remnant of the giants" (Rephaim) (Deut 3:11; Josh 12:4, 5; 13:12).

That this area was inhabited before the 18th century B.C. is confirmed by Glueck's surface exploration of Eastern Palestine. He reports that about 5 km east-northeast of "Jebel Siyâghah," in *Kh. Qurn el-Kibsh*, he found "large quantities of EB III-MB I sherds, indicating the presence of a large Early Bronze Age settlement of approximately 2200-1800 B.C." (1935: 111; see also 1934a: 13). Then he adds that the "history of the section of Moab in the vicinity of Jebel Siyâghah is the same as that of the rest of Moab. There was an occupation between 2200-1800 B.C., followed by a blank period extending down to the 13th century B.C. when only roaming Bedouin peopled the land" (1935: 111).[48]

The Rephaim are believed by some commentators to have been the builders of many megalithic monuments found in Transjordan. There are dolmens, boulders with little chambers, menhirs, and also stone circles and heaps of stones in great quantities. The stone circles and the heaps of stones can be of later date (in fact, many are quite recent) (Saller and Bagatti 1949: 17-18).[49] But the date of the dolmens is still unsettled, ranging from the Neolithic Period to the Middle Bronze Age (Saller and Bagatti 1949: 17).[50] According to Conder, "in Gilead and Moab there are probably more than a thousand dolmens, and many other rude-stone monuments" (1892: 271). There is a "great dolmen centre on the ridge west of Sihon's city . . ." (1892: 142). There are many others in the south of the Nebo region which have been interpreted as altars (Saller and Bagatti 1949: 16), but the most common opinion is that they were tombs (Saller and Bagatti 1949: 16; Horn 1960: 909-910).

Conder also reports the existence of "large boulders or fallen crags . . . near the dolmen groups," "at Hesbân, Sûmieh, Nebo, Mareighât, and elsewhere" (1892: 267). Each boulder is "pierced with a little chamber, generally about 3 feet [0.90 m] square, and 5 feet [1.50 m] long" (1892: 267-268). He suggests that these might be the "real graves of the dolmen builders," but recognizes that their small size is puzzling (1892: 268). The menhirs are dated "like the dolmens" (Saller and Bagatti 1949: 19).

In the fortieth year of the Exodus (*cf.* Num 20:23-29; 33:38), Israel was about to cross the River Arnon. At that time the land north of the Arnon was ruled by Sihon, king of the Amorites, with Heshbon as his capital city (Num 21:26). Numbers 21:26-30 can be understood as saying that Sihon had rather recently driven the Moabites from Heshbon to the south of the Arnon River.[51] It is not known for how long the region had belonged to Moab before Sihon conquered it. But evidently the Moabites were well-established there, because even after the defeat of Sihon by Moses: (a) the plain on the eastern side of the Jordan River, across from Jericho, is called "plains of Moab";[52] (b) Balak's and Balaam's intervention takes place in Sihon's former territory (Num 22-24); (c) "the people began to commit whoredom with the daughters of Moab" (Num 25:1) in the plains of Moab across from Jericho; and (d) Moses died and was buried "in the land of Moab" (Deut 34:5, 6).

"Frequently the W. el-Heshbân-er-Râmeh was the northern boundary of the land of Moab, but at certain times the Moabite territory stretched as far n. as the W. Nimrîn" (Glueck 1951: 366-367), "the northern boundary of the עַרְבוֹת מוֹאָב" (Van Zyl 1960: 59; cf. 113).

Abel, based on Deut 2:19, 37, Josh 13:25 and Judg 11:13, 15, believes that even before the Moabite settlement the Ammonites occupied the territory from the Arnon to the Jabbok, and from the desert to the Jordan and the Dead Sea. The Ammonites would have been pushed to the east by the advancing Amorites (Abel 1933: 277). Van Zyl adds that after the Amorites had conquered the region up to the Arnon, Moabitic tribes moved north of the Arnon and started controlling that territory. Finally, when their influence became strong, the Amorites reacted under the command of Sihon, and recaptured the area. "The song of mockery refers to this campaign of the Amorites against the Moabites" (1960: 113-114).[53]

Combining Abel and Van Zyl's viewpoints, the sequence of domination of the region would be as follows: Ammonites—Amorites—Moabites—Amorites—Israelites. But there are some problems posed by these views.

The expression "half of the land of the children of Ammon" (assigned to Gad, according to Josh 13:25) refers undoubtedly to the western half of the Ammonite territory conquered by the Amorites, north of Heshbon. It is very improbable that their territory reached to the Arnon in the south (Simons 1959: 120), as Abel claims. The very fact that the expression "half the land of the children of Ammon" is used only when giving the borders of Gad's territory (and not of Reuben's)[54] supports the idea that the Ammonites had occupied only the northern half of the Belqa.[55] As has already been presented, the Moabite influence was very strong in the southern Belqa at the time of the Exodus, and there is no evidence that the Ammonites reached any farther than W. Hesban or its vicinity before the Amorites conquered the region (Simons 1959: 120).

There is no biblical evidence to support Van Zyl's contention that Sihon's campaign was made to recapture Amorite territory previously lost to the Moabites. After the Rephaim and before Sihon (Num 21:26-30; cf. Deut 2:9, 10, 19-21), only the Moabites appear clearly in the biblical record as connected with the southern Belqa, and specifically, with Heshbon.

Sihon's territory extended from the Arnon to the Jabbok, and from the Ammonite border in the east to the Jordan River and the Dead Sea in the west (Num 21:23, 24; Josh 12:2, 5; 13:10; cf. Deut 2:34-36).[56]

From the Israelite Conquest to Solomon
(ca. 1400-931 B.C.)

Circa 1400 B.C., Moses defeated Sihon, king of the Amorites who dwelt in Heshbon (Num 21:21-26, 34; Deut 1:3, 4; 2:24; 3:2, 6; 29:7; Josh 9:10; 12:2, 5; 13:10, 21, 27; Neh 9:22; etc.). His territory was given as an inheritance to the tribes of Reuben and Gad (Num 32; Josh 13:15-28).

Heshbon was given to the tribe of Reuben (Josh 13:15, 17). But it seems to have been on the very border of the territories of Reuben and Gad (Josh 13:26). Reuben's territory went as far south as the Arnon, and from the desert and the Ammonite border in the east to the Jordan River and the Dead Sea in the west (Abel 1938: 69).

Numbers 32:37, 38 reports that "the children of Reuben built Heshbon, and Elealeh . . . and gave other names unto the cities which they builded." But the border between the territories of Reuben and Gad seems to have been rather imprecise. According to Num 32:34-36, among the cities built by "the children of Gad" are Ataroth and Dibon. These cities were located in the southern half of the territory attributed to Reuben.[57] Very soon, still in Joshua's lifetime, Heshbon appears as part of the territory of Gad, being mentioned as one of the four cities assigned to the Levites of the family of Merari (Josh 21:38, 39).[58] Later, the Gadites expanded further to the north and the south (1 Chr 5:11, 16).

During the early period of the judges, about 1316 B.C. (Horn 1960: 205), Eglon, king of Moab, allied with the Ammonites and the Amalekites, "sent and smote Israel, and possessed the city of palm trees" (Judg 3:13). If he occupied even Jericho, it can be assumed that Heshbon and the surrounding country were also taken. Eighteen years later (Judg 3:14-30), Ehud crossed the Jordan and killed Eglon. The residence of the Moabite king seems to have been "not far across the Jordan from Gilgal" (Nichol 1954a: 325, 327). Although the biblical record does not say it, it can be assumed that Heshbon and the surrounding country fell again into the hands of the Israelites. Otherwise Jephthah's statement (ca. 1100 B.C.) that "Israel dwelt in Heshbon and her towns . . . three hundred years" (Judg 11:26) would not be very meaningful.

Then, in Judg 11, the situation has changed. Jephthah tried to negotiate a peaceful settlement with "the king of the children of Ammon" (Judg 11:13-28) about the territory that Israel had occupied for three hundred years. Since (a) Chemosh, the national god of the Moabites, is mentioned as "thy God" (Judg 11:24) (i.e., the god of the king of the Ammonites); and (b) the disputed territory extended, according to the

Ammonite king, "from Arnon even unto Jabbok, and unto Jordan" (Judg 11:13), it can be assumed that Ammonites and Moabites appear united here, the latter probably as subjects of the former. An Ammonite king rules over "the land of Moab" and "the land of the children of Ammon" (Judg 11:15; *cf.* vss. 13, 33).

In the war following between Jephthah and the Ammonites, Jephthah gained a great victory. Although the names given in Judg 11:33 cannot be located with absolute certainty, it is very possible that the liberation reached Heshbon. Minnith, mentioned there (*cf.* Ezek 27:17), is thought to have been near Heshbon, and "the plain of the vineyards" (or Abel-Cheramim) has been identified with two possible sites close to modern Amman (Nichol 1954a: 377).

King Saul (1050-1011) fought successful wars against the Moabites and Ammonites (1 Sam 14:47). But during his reign the border between Moab and Israel was ill-defined, with Heshbon lying in the disputed territory (Kraeling 1956: 237, map 7: EFG-4).

David (1011-971) "smote Moab" and subdued it (2 Sam 8:2, 11, 12; 1 Chr 18:2). Evidently he pushed the border south to the Arnon, because when the census was taken, they started from that river to the north (2 Sam 24:5; *cf.* Josh 13:16; Abel 1938: 77; Simons 1959: 116-117, n. 78). It is interesting to notice that the Arnon is mentioned in the text as "the river of Gad."

Solomon (971-931) mentions[59] "the fishpools of Heshbon, by the gate of Bath-rabbim."[60] Heshbon appears here as a city with some splendor. It was located in the last district mentioned in the list of twelve that "provided victuals for the king and his household" during Solomon's reign (1 Kgs 4:7-19).

From the Division of the Kingdom to the Syro-Ephraimite War (931-734 B.C.)

After the breakup of the kingdom (931), Heshbon fell into the territory of Israel. Moab seems to have regained then a measure of independence. But Omri (885-874) subjugated Moab again and exacted a high annual tribute (2 Kgs 3:4).[61] But after the death of Ahab (874-853), Mesha, king of Moab, rebelled against Israel (2 Kgs 1:1; 3:4, 5). Jehoram (852-841), with the help of Jehoshaphat of Judah and a king of Edom, went against the Moabites (2 Kgs 3). In spite of their victory over them (2 Kgs 3:24, 25), they could not capture the king. It seems that at this time, King Mesha extended his territory to the north. In the Moabite Stone he claims to have conquered cities and places like Ataroth, Dibon, Madaba, and Nebo. This would place his northern border just south and southwest of Heshbon (Lombardi 1963: col. 1214). Some scholars believe that the Moabite Stone records events that happened between Mesha's revolt and Jehoram's campaign (Heidet 1903: col. 661; Smith 1902: 567-568).

Under Jehu's reign (841-814) an invasion of Hazael of Damascus is recorded (2 Kgs 10:32, 33). He smote "the land of Gilead, the Gadites, and the Reubenites,

and the Manassites, from Aroer, which is by the river Arnon, even Gilead and Bashan." It seems clear that Israel, under Jehu, had pushed the Moabites back to their traditional northern border (Arnon River), as the Syrians are said to have smitten Israelite territory here (*cf.* Van Zyl 1960: 145-146).

Evidently the Moabites tried again later to push their border to the north. Bands of Moabites "invaded the land" (2 Kgs 13:20) at the time of Elisha's death (beginning of the 8th century). Some years later, Jeroboam II (sole ruler 782-753) is credited with having "restored the coast of Israel from the entering of Hamath unto the sea of the plain" (2 Kgs 14:25). Comparing this statement with Amos 6:13, 14 and Isa 15:7, Simons concludes that the southern limit was the *W. el-Hesā* (1959: 105). If this is so, Heshbon was again in the hands of the kings of Israel. Van Zyl (1960: 147-148) thinks, however, that the southern limit must have been "not at the southern end" of the Dead Sea. "Perhaps it may be identified with the W. el-Kefrein." According to him, the territory south of W. Kefrein "was given to Uzziah as compensation for the help rendered by him" (to Jeroboam II).[62]

Three passages seem to support Van Zyl's position: (a) 2 Chr 26:8: "And the Ammonites gave gifts to Uzziah" (*i.e.*, paid tribute, this would be strange if Israel controlled the whole region); (b) 2 Chr 27:7: Jotham (750-731), son of Uzziah, "fought also with the king of the Ammonites," who, apparently, had stopped sending "gifts"; and (c) 1 Chr 5:17 mentions Jotham of Judah and Jeroboam II in relation with Transjordan, and particularly with the children of Gad (vss. 11-17).

From the texts just referred to it can be inferred that during Uzziah's reign the Ammonites bought their independence from Judah by paying tribute. Evidently that tribute was not paid later, perhaps after Uzziah's death, and so Jotham conducted a military campaign against Ammon. Adding to this analysis 1 Chr 5:11, 16, it can be inferred also that Gadites still occupied the territory of Gad. But the Gadites had expanded to the north, adding some Manassite territory in "Bashan unto Salchah",[63] and also to the south "in all the suburbs of Sharon."[64] Sharon means "flat country" and is virtually equivalent to Mishor. So here it could stand for the Mishor of Reuben (Simons 1959: 123). This, together with the Moabite Stone (a century before),[65] would point to a southward expansion of Gad.

The texts just quoted do not make any reference to Judah's control of Heshbon proper. But if Judah controlled Ammon, it is not unlikely that she also had some control over the territory between Ammon and Judah.

In any case, Judah's control of that part of Transjordan did not last very long. According to 2 Kgs 16:6, after vainly attempting to take Jerusalem—at the beginning of the Syro-Ephraimite War—Rezin, king of Syria, "recovered Elath." There is no mention of the route he used to reach that far-away place, but the most natural thing for the king of Syria would have been to follow the "king's highway" (of Transjordan) that passed by Heshbon. But, since he was already in western Palestine, he could have proceeded also from Jerusalem to the south.

From the Syro-Ephraimite War to Cyrus' Capture of Babylon (734-539 B.C.)

As a result of the Syro-Ephraimite War (2 Kgs 16:5-9; cf. Isa 7:1-9; Nichol 1954a: 85-86, 1955: 131), Ahaz (735-715) bought the help of Tiglath-pileser III against these immediate foes. According to the Eponym Canon, Tiglath-pileser III attacked Philistia in 734 B.C. (Nichol 1954a: 941; Thomas 1965: 53). He probably clashed also with Israel (Van Zyl 1960: 149).

The Assyrian intervention was apparently used by Salamanu[66] of Moab to extend his territory north of the Arnon. If he is the Shalman of Hos 10:14, and if Beth-arbel is the "Arbela" of Eusebius[67], then there would be a reference here to a Moabite invasion that reached farther north than any of the historical borders of Moab.

In 733-732 Tiglath-pileser resumed his campaign in Syria-Palestine. He took Damascus, occupied the greater part of Galilee and Gilead, and deported their inhabitants. In 1 Chr 5:26 mention is made of "the Reubenites, and the Gadites, and the half tribe of Manasseh" and of their being carried away.

According to the "Slab Inscription" of Nimrud (Thomas 1965: 56; cf. Van Zyl 1960: 149, n. 9), Salamanu paid tribute to Tiglath-pileser and so "prevented the Assyrian army from entering his territory" (Van Zyl 1960: 149). The situation seems to have remained so for some years. In a letter that Mallowan found in Calah, it is stated that the Moabites and a few other nations sent horses to one or another of the following Assyrian kings: Tiglath-pileser III (745-727), Shalmaneser V (727-722), and Sargon II (722-705) (Van Zyl 1960: 149-150, n. 9).

Samaria's fall (722 B.C.) was happy news for the Moabites. Van Zyl sees in Isa 15-16 remnants of a mocking song, quoted by Isaiah, with prophetical additions and warnings, intended to discourage Judah from relying on Moab in revolting against Assyria (1960: 20-23, 150). As extrabiblical proof of this revolt he mentions the Clay Prism of Sargon II. The revolt, the prism states, took place in the ninth year of Sargon. Since the revolt was suppressed in 711 B.C., it must have lasted for about three years (Van Zyl 1960: 150). Moab "hastened to pay homage to the Assyrian king and as Sargon regained control of the main route by subjecting Ashdod, he did not try to capture the more remote territories of Judah, Ammon and Moab" (Van Zyl 1960: 150). In 701 B.C., when Hezekiah tried to throw off the Assyrian yoke, Moab and other surrounding countries seem to have remained loyal to Assyria (cf. Isa 30:1-5; 31:1-3; 2 Kgs 19:9; 20:12-19).

Besides Salamanu, who paid tribute to Tiglath-pileser III, the following Moabite kings are known from Assyrian records: Kammusunadbi (Pritchard 1950: 287)

(under Sennacherib [705-681]), Musuri and Kamashaltu (Pritchard 1950: 291, 294, 298) (under Esarhaddon [681-669] and Ashurbanipal [669-ca. 627]).

So, from ca. 733 B.C., until the reign of Ashurbanipal, at least, Heshbon and the surrounding country were in Moabite hands[68], ruled by Moabite kings[69] who were Assyrian vassals. Moab paid an annual tribute of one mina of gold.[70] Nothing is known about Moab's attitude toward Assyria after Ashurbanipal.

Isaiah's prophecy against Moab, in chapters 15 and 16, belongs, undoubtedly, to the first part of the Moabite domination of this region. Together with Heshbon (Isa 15:4; 16:8, 9), other important cities north of the Arnon are attributed to Moab: Dibon, Madaba, Elealeh, etc. Heshbon appears here as a once prosperous agricultural center. Mention is made of its "fields," "summer fruits," and "harvest." The "vine of Sibmah" is also closely connected with it (cf. Nichol 1955: 176-177).

When Nebuchadnezzar first campaigned in Palestine (605 B.C.), the Moabites apparently paid him tribute and were still friendly to him for several years. They appear sometime between 602 and 598 B.C., with bands of Chaldeans, Syrians, and Ammonites, harassing the rebellious Jehoiakim, in a clearly pro-Babylonian attitude (2 Kgs 24:1, 2). But the situation was to change. Jeremiah's prophecy against Moab (Jer 48), tentatively dated between 605/04 and 594/93 (Nichol 1955: 348),[71] lists a number of Moabite cities that were going to fall under the scourge of the Babylonians. Of the 21 places named that can be identified with reasonable certainty, all but four were located to the north of the Arnon. Heshbon has a prominent place (Jer 48:2, 34, 45).

But in Jer 49:3 Heshbon appears as an Ammonite city. Jer 49 was written probably shortly after Jer 48. It is not known how, nor exactly when, the borderline was changed. Ezekiel 25:9, 10, tentatively dated ca. 588 B.C. (Nichol 1955: 572), has been interpreted as prophesying an invasion of Moab by the "men of the east"—from the desert, east of that territory—"on top of" (עֶל) "the earlier penetration of the land by the 'Ammonites'" (Simons 1959: 454; cf. Abel 1938: 123). The start of Ammonite control of Heshbon and the surrounding country can be dated about 595 B.C.

Josephus (Ant. 10.9.7) writes that Nebuchadnezzar in the 23rd year of his reign (582 B.C.) made an expedition against Coelesyria and "made war against the Ammonites and Moabites." There must have been a previous rebellion. Jeremiah (48:7) had prophesied that Chemosh, his priests, and his princes would be taken into captivity. This took place, evidently, at this time. The Ammonites also were told that their king,[72] "his priests and his princes" would go into captivity (Jer 49:3), and would "not be remembered among the nations" (Ezek 25:7, 10).

It is not known if Heshbon was destroyed or not by the victorious Chaldeans, but it was most probably sacked (Heidet 1903: col. 662).

After the destruction of the kingdoms of Ammon and Moab, the "children of the east," the Bedouins, freely entered the land (Isa 11:14; Ezek 25:9). This infiltration of Arabian elements made this region considered more as part of Arabia. It was later to become part of the Nabatean kingdom (Abel 1933: 280).

For the next three centuries, the available information about Heshbon and the surrounding country is very fragmentary. In fact, the only mention of the city of Heshbon by name, after Jer 49 and before the 2nd century B.C., is found in Neh 9:22, and here only in a historical allusion to its conquest in the time of Moses.

During the Persian Period (539-332 B.C.)

During the Persian Period, Palestine belonged to the fifth satrapy, whose capital was Damascus (Abel 1938: 115, 125; Avi-Yonah 1977: 11-12). According to Herodotus, the fifth satrapy included all the country from the city of Posidium (modern Basit in northern Syria) to the borders of Egypt. "All Phoenicia, Palestine, Syria and Cyprus, were herein contained," excluding the district "which belonged to Arabia and was free of tax" (*History* 3.89-91). The satrapy was called officially *Ebirnâri*, "the land beyond the river" (Heb. ʿEber ha-nahar, Aram. ʿAbar-nahara) (Avi-Yonah 1977: 12; *cf.* Neh 2:7, 9; Ezra 8:36; 4:10, 11, 17, 20, etc.).

The satrapy was divided into provinces (singular, *medînah*), each one presided over by a *pihat*. The provinces were, in turn, divided into districts (Heb. *pelakhim*). The districts consisted of one or two principal localities,

and a number of villages, which were the lowest administrative unit. In addition to the governorates, each satrapy included a number of cities or regions ruled by local dynasties, as well as territories of tribes, some of them semi-independent, royal fortresses, etc. (Avi-Yonah 1977: 12).

The province of Judah is mentioned in the book of Nehemiah. In the same book we find allusions to four other regions that could have been provinces also (Avi-Yonah 1977: 23): Samaria (Neh 2:10; 3:34), Ammon (Neh 2:10, 19), Arabia (Neh 2:19; 16:1), and Ashdod (Neh 4:7).

"Tobiah the servant, the Ammonite" (Neh 2:10, 19) appears to have been an influential man both in Transjordan and in Judah (Neh 6:17, 19). Several contemporary scholars believe that he was a Jew (not half Ammonite and half Jew) (Mazar 1957: 143-144; McCown 1957: 63, 72; Avi-Yonah 1977: 26). It is a fact that he was married to a Jewess, and that one of his sons also married a Jewish girl (Neh 6:17, 18). His title "the servant" might imply the idea of "servant of the king." It was used to designate government officials (*cf.* Mazar 1957: 144; McCown 1957: 71-72). Tobiah could have been, then, a government official, a "commander," or perhaps the "governor" of the province of Ammon. He is believed to have been the ancestor of the Hellenistic Tobiads who also ruled in Transjordan (Mazar 1957: 143; McCown 1957: 74-76).

If Tobiah was governor of Ammon, what were the borders of his territory? There are no clear references in the available sources. The last time that the Ammonites appear geographically located, they are mentioned in Ezek 25:1-10 as occupying Rabbah and most of the Moabite territory north of the Arnon. It is not impossible that under Tobiah, Ammon included that area, plus the country around Rabbath-Ammon (Wright and Filson 1956: pl. 7D).

The next time that the Tobiads are mentioned is in the 3rd century B.C. What happened to this region in the intervening 150 years? There is a complete gap in the available information. Since the Tobiads reappear in the 3rd century in the same location, it can be assumed that they remained there, as rulers, all of the time. But this is not certain.

Esbus[73] in Hellenistic, Maccabean, Roman, and Byzantine Times

Esbus in Hellenistic Times (332-*ca.* 164 B.C.)

When Alexander the Great took over Syria and Palestine,[74] he did not introduce major administrative changes. After his brief stay there in 332-331 B.C., he replaced the Persian satrap at Damascus by a Macedonian, Parmenio, who was followed in rapid succession by Andromachus, Menon, Ariames, Asclepiodorus, and Bessus (Avi-Yonah 1977: 32).[75] The titles of the rulers were changed to the Greek (*cf.* Diodorus 1958: 1).

After changing hands several times in the wars between Alexander's successors, Syria-Palestine came firmly into the hands of the Ptolemies in 301 B.C. As pointed out by Avi-Yonah, "the whole area under Ptolemaic rule in Asia was officially called Syria and Phoenicia but in common usage there prevailed the unofficial 'Coele-Syria'" (Avi-Yonah 1977: 33). In this region the basic political subdivision was the *hyparchy*. This was, thus, a secondary administrative unit, corresponding with the Persian *medinah* or "province" within a satrapy. Hyparchies were, in turn, subdivided into tertiary units carrying the name *toparchy* and paralleling the Persian *pelekh* or "district" (consisting of a group of villages). "The Greek colonies established within a hyparchy seem to have remained within its administrative framework," Avi-Yonah points out. "They were not exempted from its jurisdiction, unless granted the special status of a *polis*" (1977: 34).

In western and southern Palestine the hyparchies of Galilee, Samaria, Judaea, Ashdod, and Idumaea were administrative units based largely on the earlier subdivisions of the territory (Avi-Yonah 1977: 35-38). East of the Jordan, however, both the subdividing of the larger territories into smaller units and the establishment of Greek colonies found more favorable ground, as that region was for the most part less-densely populated (see Avi-Yonah 1977: 39).[76] Specifically, "the Hauran was now divided into the districts of

Trachonitis and Auranitis, Karnaim into Batanea (biblical Bashan), Gaulanitis (the biblical Golan), and the territory of the city of Dium"; and Gilead was reduced to Galaaditis, after taking from it the territories of Pella and Gerasa. "Philadelphia ('Ammân) was made independent of Tobiad rule" (Avi-Yonah 1977: 40).

The Zenon papyri (Mazar 1957: 139),[77] of the time of Ptolemy II Philadelphus (285-246), give a prominent place to the Tobiads in Transjordan during this period, particularly to one Tobiah. He, in letters exchanged with King Ptolemy II and his minister of finance Apollonius,[78] appears as an autonomous ruler of his own land, swearing loyalty to the king of Egypt. He commanded a military "cleruchy."[79] His territory is mentioned, in another document, as 'εν τη Τουβιου,[80] that is, in the land of Tobiah. A contract was written in 259 B.C. in Βιρτα της 'Αμμανιτιδος,[81] "Birta of this Ammonitis." This Βιρτα is undoubtedly the same Τυρος (Aram. Bîrthâ), the stronghold of the Tobiads mentioned by Josephus (Ant. 12.4.11). Its impressive ruins are still visible today at 'Araq el-Emîr, fourteen and a half miles west-southwest of Amman (Horn 1960: 1106).[82]

The territory ruled by the Tobiads did not include Philadelphia (mentioned as an autonomous city, with its ancient name: 'Εν Ραββαταμμανοις) on the east (Mazar 1957: 142). On the south its border was probably the W. Hesban, which was at the same time the northern border of the Moabites (Mazar 1957: 142; Avi-Yonah 1977: 41). Josephus says that in the 2nd century B.C. Tyre (of the Tobiads) was located "between Arabia and Judea, beyond Jordan, not far from the country of Heshbon" (Ant. 12.4.11).[83] Here Esbus appears to be the center of a district. But later, according to Josephus, Esbus was among the cities of Moabitis (Ant. 13.15.4). Since Esbus is the first city mentioned as part of Moabitis, perhaps it was its capital and at times its name was applied to the whole district. Moabitis and Gabalitis (or Gamalitis), both south of Ammonitis, were disputed between the Ptolemies and the Nabateans (Avi-Yonah 1977: 41).

During the 3rd century B.C., the Seleucids fought four unsuccessful wars with the Ptolemies for the control of Syria-Palestine.[84] However, in 198 B.C., when Antiochus III defeated the Egyptian army at Paneas, the territory of "Syria and Phoenicia" came under Seleucid control. The Seleucid rule lasted, in theory at least, until 104 B.C., though around Esbus in Transjordan its effective control ended before 164 B.C.

Antiochus III organized territory conquered from the Ptolemies into a new strategia (a primary administrative unit equivalent to the Persian satrapy) and called it "Coele-Syria and Phoenicia." Syria to the north was one strategia named "Seleucis" (Avi-Yonah 1977: 44).[85]

"Coele-Syria and Phoenicia" was divided into just four eparchies, units larger than the Ptolemaic hyparchies: Samaria, Idumaea, Paralia (the coastal plain), and Galaaditis (all of the region east of the Jordan, except Peraea). The earlier hyparchies that

were left without ethnarchy status in this new administrative structure would be subject to the ethnarch of one of the ethnarchies. Thus, as stated by Avi-Yonah, "All the other provinces, which may possibly have retained their former designation of hyparchy, were reduced to tertiary units from their previous status of secondary ones" (Avi-Yonah 1977: 46; cf. 47-50).

Peraea, then as well as Judaea, were subject to the ethnarch of Samaria, and were even after Judaea had been given the status of a separate eparchy. The rest of Transjordan constituted the eparchy of Galaaditis. Esbus was left in Moabitis, only a few miles from the border of Peraea (Avi-Yonah 1977: 48, 50; map 3).

Esbus in Maccabean-Hasmonean Times
(ca. 164-63 B.C.)

The situation of Transjordan, south of Moabitis, remained fluid. It had been so since the Persian Period. The Nabateans and other Arabs were advancing toward the north. Hyrcanus, grandson of the 3rd-century Tobiah, while living in his family's estate called Tyre (181-175 B.C.), warred against the Arabs (Josephus Ant. 12.4.11; Abel 1938: 136-137). A few years later (ca. 164 B.C.) Judas Maccabeus found the Nabateans in Galaad. His brothers Jonathan, Simon, and John made contact with them too, and also encountered in Madaba the unfriendly sons of Jambri who killed John (ca. 160 B.C.).[86] The Nabatean hold on Transjordan was to become larger and stronger in the next two and a half centuries.

It is evident from 1 Macc 5:26, 36 that there was a rather strong Jewish settlement in Transjordan during the middle of the 2nd century B.C. The Maccabeans extended their territory in that direction, gaining at least de facto control in the time of Jonathan Maccabeus (160-143/42 B.C.), and possibly even de jure control over a portion of the territory if one of the four nomes granted Jonathan by Antiochus VI was Peraea, as seems likely (see Avi-Yonah 1977: 54-57).

When John Hyrcanus I (135-105/04 B.C.), the son of Simon Maccabeus, heard of the death of Antiochus VII Sidetes (129 B.C.), he attacked and captured the cities of Madaba and Samaga. It seems surprising that Esbus is not mentioned as well; but most probably it was also added at this time, for it is mentioned later among the cities of Moab that were in Jewish hands at the beginning of the reign of Alexander Jannaeus (103-76/75 B.C.) (Josephus Ant. 13.9.1, 13.15.5; Avi-Yonah 1977: 57).

Alexander Jannaeus succeeded in making the Dead Sea a Jewish Sea. It was during his reign, and in any event not earlier than that of John Hyrcanus, that the country was divided into the "lands" of Judaea, Idumaea, Samaria, Galilee, and Peraea (Josephus Wars 3.3.1-5). The internal administration of this Hasmonean State is, unfortunately, not well known. It seems that the districts were administered by governors who in the Greek sources carried the title of strategos or *meridarchēs* (1 Macc 16:11; Josephus *Ant.* 14.1.3). As for the "Greek cities taken by Jannaeus and the districts conquered in Moab," these seem "to have remained under military rule outside the normal district administration" (Avi-Yonah 1977: 73).

Meanwhile, during Jannaeus' reign the Nabateans had been advancing northward, and Jannaeus was defeated by Obedas I in the Gaulan or Gilead, *ca.* 90 B.C., and again later by Aretas III (*ca.* 85-*ca.* 60 B.C.). The Nabateans occupied Coele-Syria and its capital, Damascus, but nevertheless Jannaeus retained the conquered territory in Moabitis.[87]

Under Alexandra (76/75-67 B.C.), Jannaeus' widow and successor, no territorial changes occurred.[88] After her death there ensued a civil war led by her two sons, Aristobulus II and Hyrcanus II. Hyrcanus II, in order to secure Nabatean help to overcome his brother, agreed to deliver twelve cities in Moab to Aretas III.[89] Esbus is not listed among the twelve, but will appear again in the records as a military colony of Herod the Great (Josephus *Ant.* 15.8.5). Avi-Yonah suggests, "It could have remained in Jewish hands throughout, or it could have been ceded by Hyrcanus II and retaken by Herod after his victory over the Arabs" (1977: 77 n. 3).

It was during the civil strife between Aristobulus II and Hyrcanus II that the Roman general Pompey reached Syria and Palestine with a Roman army. Jerusalem was taken in 63 B.C.

Esbus in Roman Times (63 B.C.-A.D. 330)[90]

When Pompey took Jerusalem, he put an end to the independent Hasmonean kingdom and also took considerable territory away from Judaea, allowing Hyrcanus II to continue as high priest and rule with the title of ethnarch, probably under the supervision of the Roman governor of the new province of Syria.

In Transjordan, Pompey created a league of Greek cities, the *Decapolis*, whose southernmost city was Philadelphia. The status of Esbus is unknown between the time of Aristobulus II (67-63 B.C.) and Herod the Great (37-4 B.C.). It may have been in Nabatean hands, as indicated by Avi-Yonah (1977: 83, map 5),[91] but could have been relatively unimportant to the Nabateans, whose main interests in the area lay with the trade route farther east, as suggested by Larry Mitchel.[92] This may account for the lack of reference to it in the sources during this period.

Herod the Great ruled over Judaea, Idumaea, Samaria, Galilee, and Peraea, plus several Hellenized cities. A *meridarchēs*, or governor, headed each of these five major divisions.[93]

In order to fortify his kingdom, Herod built or rebuilt several fortresses and fortified cities. Among these we find, as "built," Ἐσεβωνίτιν in Peraea (Josephus *Ant.* 15.8.5). It is not clear what the full meaning of "built" is in this context. It could just mean that Herod fortified the city.[94] He placed veterans there, probably in order to protect his frontier with the

Nabateans (Josephus *Ant.* 15.8.5). As indicated above, Esbus was under Herod and was within Peraea. Nevertheless, it probably enjoyed the semiautonomous status of a *polis*, due undoubtedly to its preeminently military importance (Avi-Yonah 1977: 99; *cf.* 94).

Herod fought against the Nabateans, and was at first defeated by Malichos I (60-30 B.C.) (Abel 1938: 149).[95] Then, however, he decisively defeated the Nabateans near Philadelphia (32-31 B.C.) (Schürer, First Div. 2: 356). The defeated Nabateans, Josephus claims, made Herod the ruler (προστατης) of their nation (*Ant.* 15.5.1-5; *cf.* Abel 1938: 145-150).

After Herod's death, his son Herod Antipas (4 B.C.-A.D. 39) received Galilee, Peraea, and the title of tetrarch. But Esbus apparently did not stay in Herod Antipas' hands. The fact is that the Ἐσεβωνίτιδι appears later on, in Josephus, east of Peraea, together with Arabia, Philadelphia, and Gerasa.[96] It was a town district, distinct from Peraea and also from Arabia, but perhaps subject to the Arabians (Nabateans) (Schürer, Second Div. 1: 129-130).

Most probably Esbus fell into Nabatean hands after the death of Herod the Great (Schürer, Second Div. 1: 129-130; *cf.* Avi-Yonah 1977: 103, map 7). Several facts point in this direction: (a) Machaerus fell, at least temporarily, under Nabatean control, during the reign of Herod Antipas (Josephus *Ant.* 18.5.1); (b) Nabatean inscriptions make known some Nabatean strategoi (district rulers) that ruled in Madaba and *Umm el-Reṣāṣ* during the 1st century A.D. (Abel 1938: 165); (c) Pliny speaks of the Arabs *Esbonitae*, a designation that could be taken as only ethnical,[97] or could have some relation to Esbus (Pliny says that their border "adjoins the frontier of Syria") (Plinius Secundus *Nat. Hist.* 5.12); (d) at the outbreak of the Jewish war (A.D. 66), insurgent Jews sacked "Heshbon and its district" (Josephus *Wars* 2.18.1);[98] and (e) when in A.D. 106 the Nabatean kingdom came to its end, and the province of Arabia was established by the Romans, Esbus was included in this province (Abel 1938: 349). All of these facts do not conclusively prove that Esbus was in Nabatean hands since the reign of Herod Antipas, but they do make a strong case for such a thesis.

As already mentioned, at the beginning of the Jewish war in A.D. 66, the Jews sacked Esbus (Josephus *Wars* 2.18.1). Perhaps more than the city of Esbus is intended here because the name appears as Ἐσεβωνίτιν giving rather the idea of the district of Esbus.[99] During the course of the war (A.D. 66-70) the Jews created several military commands: Judaea, Idumaea, the coastal plain, Galilee, Peraea, and Jericho and the toparchies of Gophna and Acraba (Josephus *Wars* 2.20.3-6; see Avi-Yonah 1977: 107). According to Josephus, "the whole of Peraea as far as Machaerus either surrendered or was subdued" by the Roman general Placidus (Josephus *Wars* 4.7.6). Esbus was undoubtedly included in this pacification.

After the Jewish War, Judaea was made into an independent province, ruled by a governor of senatorial rank, who was a propraetor entitled "legate." The legion *Decima Fretensis* was placed under his command (Avi-Yonah 1977: 107; *cf.* Lifshitz 1969: 458-160). Urbanization became a characteristic policy inasmuch as the municipalities had been generally peaceful during the war. Virtually the whole country eventually became "city-territories" or "city-areas." "Vespasian restored autonomous municipal status to some cities which had possessed it under Pompey and his successors, but had subsequently become part of Herod's domain" (Avi-Yonah 1977: 111).

Excluded either temporarily or permanently from this city-area organizational pattern were the following: a region around Jerusalem, Upper Galilee, the Gaulan, Jericho, and a portion of Transjordan. "Jericho and the three districts of Peraea," Avi-Yonah points out, "were set aside as imperial estates" (1977: 112).

In A.D. 105, the legate of Syria, following orders from Emperor Trajan, occupied the Nabatean territory, and on March 22, 106, the Nabatean kingdom was turned into the Roman province of Arabia, administered by a praetorian legate (Abel 1938: 165). Its first capital was Petra, and its garrison was the *Legio III Cyrenaica*, stationed at Bostra (Avi-Yonah 1977: 113; Abel 1938: 165).[100]

In Ptolemy's *Geography* (5.17), which reflects the political geography of *ca.* A.D. 130-*ca.* 160, Εσβουτα appears as part of *Arabia Petraea*, at 68 1/2 1/3° longitude and 31° latitude. It can be assumed that Esbus was included in this province of Arabia since its creation in A.D. 106. Gerasa, Philadelphia, and Dium were also within the new province, but there is not a complete agreement among scholars concerning the date (within the 2nd century A.D.) these cities were incorporated (Abel 1938: 167; Avi-Yonah 1977: 113).

Shortly after the creation of the Provincia Arabia, Claudius Severus, its first governor, built the *via nova* (also called *via Trajan*) from Aila (in *'Aqabah*) to Bostra, along what was possibly an earlier caravan route. The section south of Philadelphia was already in use in A.D. 111, and the northern section was ready by 114. In 129 Emperor Hadrian improved the northern section, and in 162 Marcus Aurelius improved the whole road. To the middle of the 4th century, most of the emperors (their names appear in milestone inscriptions) helped keep it in good repair (Abel 1938: 228; see Avi-Yonah 1977: 183). Esbus was located on the southern section of this road, as were also *Kh. el-Sūq*, *el-Yadūde*, Madaba, etc. (Abel 1938: 228-229).

The *via nova* is still well-preserved in some places, where it is 6 m wide. It appears slightly elevated in the middle, with a line of stones in the center and one line of stones on each side. The filling is made of basalt rubble work. The milestones are consistently limestone (Abel 1938: 228).

Around A.D. 129-130, in preparation for Emperor Hadrian's visit, a road was built to connect Esbus with Livias, Jericho, and Jerusalem (Avi-Yonah 1977: 183-184). Milestones 5-7, from Esbus, have been found

(numbered 229, 230, and 231 in fig. 1.2 [Thomsen 1917: 67-68; see Abel 1938: 223]). The first two have several inscriptions each, mentioning several Roman emperors. The inscriptions of Milestone 5 have been dated to 219, 307, 364-375(?), and 219(?). Those of Milestone 6 have been dated to 162, 236, and 288.[101]

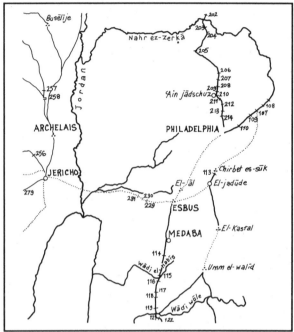

Fig. 1.2 Roman milestones found in part of the *Provincia Arabia* (after Thomsen 1917)

The Greek name 'Εσβουντος (in the phrase απο 'Εσβουντος...) appears four times in the inscriptions, and the Latin spelling *Esb[unte]* occurs once. The fact that the miles were counted from Esbus shows the relative importance of the city, and in any case implies its function as a beginning or pivotal point for the road.

Apparently the Jewish revolt led by Bar Kokhba (A.D. 132-135) did not affect the province of Arabia to any significant extent. However, the province of Judaea was renamed Syria-Palestine after the revolt was crushed (Abel 1938: 163).[102]

Some time later, Septimius Severus (193-211) reshaped somewhat the provincial geography of the entire region by transferring Auranitis from Syria to Arabia and by dividing the rest of Syria into the two provinces of Syria proper and Phoenicia (Avi-Yonah 1977: 115). Elagabalus (218-222), according to Avi-Yonah (1977: 117), raised to municipal status the cities of Characmoba (*Kerak*) and Esbus, now called officially *Aurelia Esbus* (Hill 1922: xxxiii, 29, 30, plate V, 1-3). The existence of these and other "munici-palities" is known "almost exclusively from the coins struck by them in the exercise of their municipal rights" (Avi-Yonah 1977: 117).[103]

Under Diocletian (284-304) new administrative changes affected the province of Arabia. The territory belonging to this province south of the Arnon River (W. el-Mojib) was attached to Palestine, but Trachonitis and Batanaea were, in turn, added to Arabia (Avi-Yonah 1977: 118). The military command, now separated from the civil administration, was in the hands of *dux Arabiae*, whose jurisdiction apparently reached as far south as the Zered (W. el-Hesa). The province of Arabia became one of the provinces of the diocese of the East, which in turn belonged to the prefecture of the East.[104]

Esbus in Byzantine Times (A.D. 330-640)

In the treatment of Esbus in Byzantine times, the administrative changes that affected Palestine from the 4th to the 7th centuries will be presented first; then the history and importance of Esbus will be discussed.

About A.D. 358 and again about A.D. 400 partitions of Palestine were made that resulted finally in three provinces: *Palaestina prima* (Judaea, Idumaea, Samaria, and Peraea), *Palaestina secunda* (Galilee, the Gaulan, and the cities of the Decapolis from Pella northward), and *Palaestina tertia* or *Palaestina tersiasive salutaris* (the region southward from the Arnon east of the Dead Sea and from Beersheba in western Palestine). The capital cities were, respectively, Caesarea, Scythopolis, and Petra (Avi-Yonah 1977: 121, 125; *cf.* Parkes 1949: 58). The *Notitia Dignitatum* (*ca.* A.D. 400),[105] and an edict of Theodosius II (*ca.* 409) (Avi-Yonah 1977: 121; Abel 1938: 170)[106] provide the earliest evidence for the partitions of *ca.* 400 that resulted in these three Palestines. Hierocles, in the 6th century, and Georgius Cyprius, in the 7th century, use this triple division as the basis for their city lists. The lists of bishops at the councils of Ephesus (431) and Chalcedon (451) and two provincial synods of Jerusalem (518, 536), provide additional witness to the same triple division.[107]

The *Notitia Dignitatum* provides also a list of the garrisons that were under the duke of Arabia. The *legionis tertiae Cyrenaicae* was still in Bostra. There is no mention of a garrison in Esbus (Abel 1938: 187-191).

As for ecclesiastical territories, from the time of Constantine the Great onward, these accorded closely with the civil ones. "The archbishop took up his seat in the capital of the province; each city had a bishop. In consequence, we may assume conversely that each episcopal see had municipal rights" (Avi-Yonah 1977: 122).[108] However, there were "some modifications in the course of time"; for instance, in 451 Jerusalem was given a heightened status of patriarchate (Avi-Yonah 1977: 122). Earlier, in the Council of Nicaea (325),[109] Antioch in the diocese of the East, and Alexandria in the Diocese of Egypt, had been officially recognized as patriarchal sees (Schaff and Wace 1900: 15).[110]

Esbus appears for the first time as an episcopal see at the time of the Council of Nicaea. It belonged to the province of Arabia, and its metropolitan was at Bostra. Arabia, together with Syria, Phoenicia, Cilicia, Mesopotamia, and Cyprus, were assigned to the patriarchate of Antioch (Fortescue 1907: 16).

The bishop of Esbus, Gennadius, appears twice in the acts of the Council of Nicaea. His full name and title are given first as *Gennadius Jabrudorum Ybutensis Provinciae Arabiae* (Mansi 1960a: col. 694), and then as *Gennadius Bunnorum Arabiae*.[111]

Eusebius of Caesarea (*ca.* 275-*ca.* 340), in his *Onomasticon* (84: 1-6), mentions Ἐσσεβῶν . . . καλεῖται δε νυν Ἐσβους, as ἐπισμος πολις της Ἀραβιας.[112] He points to its location 20 miles from the Jordan River in the mountains in front of Jericho (Eusebius *Onom* 84: 1-6; *cf.* also 12: 20-24; 16: 24-26).

Eusebius also gives the names of several towns or villages, with the indication of their distance in miles (Roman) from Esbus. This fact suggests that Esbus was at that time the capital of a provincial district. The towns mentioned in relation to Esbus are, as well, a help in determining the district's limits (Avi-Yonah 1977: 128). The towns named[113] and their distance from Esbus are as follows: Beelmaus, 9 miles; Dannaba, 7 miles; Eleale, 1 mile; Mannith, 4 miles; Nabo, 8 miles; and *mons Nabau*, 6 miles (Eusebius *Onom* 46: 1-2; 76: 9-12; 84: 10-13; 132: 1-2; 136: 6-13). In addition, Medaba is mentioned as lying close to Esbus (Eusebius *Onom* 128: 19-20) and Iazer as being 10 miles from Filadelfia and 15 miles from Esbus (Eusebius *Onom* 104: 13-19).[114]

Based on the previous information it can be said that the territory of Esbus bordered the territory of Madaba in the south, the territory of Philadelphia in the northeast, and the territory of Livias (of *Palaestina prima*) in the west (see fig. 1.3). "On the east, the posts of the *limes*[115] must have limited the city's territory..." (Abel 1938: 186).[116]

About A.D. 400, pilgrim Egeria (Aetheria) of Aquitania visited *Râs es-Siâghah* (Abel 1933: 379). From the right side of the church that existed there she was shown "Hesebon, which belonged to Sihon, king of the Amorrhites, and which today is called Exebon" (Egeria 1970: 69; *cf.* Newton 1926: 31). In the lists of bishops who attended the Council of Ephesus in 431, Ζωσυς Ἐσβουντος[117] is found. The same bishop, apparently, is mentioned in the acts of the Council of Chalcedon in 451, though evidently he was not present there, because his metropolitan, Bishop Constantinus of Bostra, signed for him.[118]

In this same Council of Chalcedon, Jerusalem was made a patriarchal see, as already mentioned above. Bishop Juvenal of Jerusalem (421-458) "surrendered his claim to the two Phoenicias and to Arabia, on condition of his being allowed metropolitical jurisdiction over the three Palestines...." (Schaff and Wace 1900: 19; *cf.* Fortescue 1907: 27). This comment betrays the struggle that took place between Antioch and Jerusalem during the first half of the 5th century for control of Phoenicia, Palestine, and Arabia. Antioch

Fig. 1.3   Byzantine Palestine (after Avi Yonah 1977)

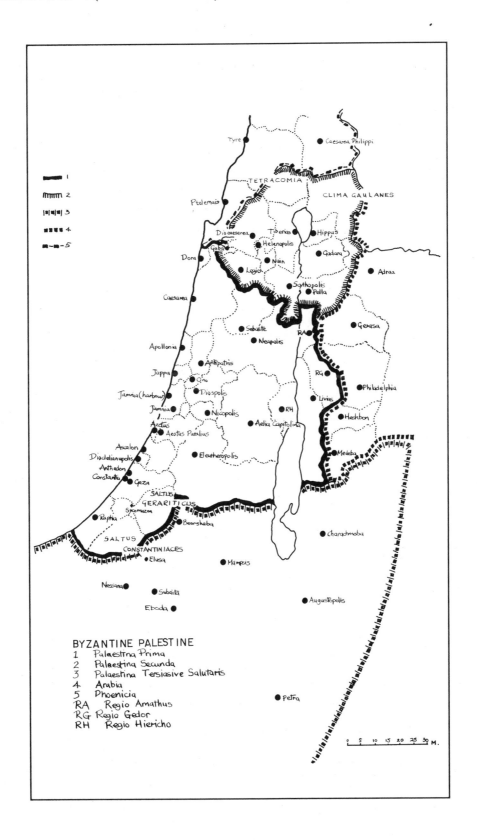

BYZANTINE PALESTINE
1   Palaestina Prima
2   Palaestina Secunda
3   Palaestina Tersiasive Salutaris
4   Arabia
5   Phoenicia
RA   Regio Amathus
RG   Regio Gedor
RH   Regio Hiericho

lost the three Palestines, and also Cyprus that century (Fortescue 1907: 16, 47-48).[119]

Thus, Esbus remained under the patriarch of Antioch, in the province of Arabia (de Vaux 1938: 254). The *Notitia Antiochena* (ca. 570) mentions *Essmos (Esbus)* still as an episcopal see, suffragan of Bostra, under Antioch, in *Bitira Arabiae* (*PL* 1855: col. 1067; see de Vaux 1938: 254).

During the excavations conducted at *Râs es-Siâghah*, a stone capital was found (in 1933), at the east end of the north aisle of the basilica. The capital is decorated with crosses, one of which has letters attached to the extremities of its arms. Read in a certain order, the letters make the word ECBY (Εσβου) (Saller 1941a: 265; 1941b: pl. 42, 2).[120] According to Abel, the buildings in *Râs es-Siâghah* originated in the course of the 4th century A.D. The basilica was started in the 5th century, destroyed in the last quarter of the 6th century, probably by an earthquake, and completely rebuilt by A.D. 597. It was used during the 7th century and probably "not entirely abandoned before the 8th" (Saller 1941a: 15, 45-46).

It is not known with certainty when this capital was made. It was, undoubtedly, part of the rebuilt basilica. "It is not improbable that the people of Esbous presented this capital to the sanctuary of Moses on Mount Nebo" (Saller 1941a: 266). This could have happened at the end of the 6th century.

According to Saller and Bagatti (1949: 147), the idea that *Siâghah*, *Mekhayat*, and *Ma'in* belonged to the diocese of Esbus is being discarded. It is now admitted that they belonged to the diocese of Madaba, at least at the end of the 6th century. Several inscriptions found in these places mentioning bishops of Madaba led to this conclusion.

A further reference to Esbus comes from Georges of Cyprus (ca. 605) in his *Descriptio orbis romani* (Salaville 1910: 298; de Vaux 1938: 249, 254).

In 1934, Mufaddi Ibn el-Haddâdin, while digging to place the foundations for his house, came across the now called "Mosaic of Ma'in" (8 km southwest of Madaba). In 1937, while trying to transform one of the rooms of the house, he uncovered fragments of it. October 14-22 of the same year, Savignac and de Vaux, of the "École Archéologique Française," uncovered whatever was still visible of the mosaic under the house and in the yard (de Vaux 1938: 227).

The mosaic, according to de Vaux, originated "in the last fourth of the sixth century or the first half of the seventh, more probably to the end of this period." It was part of a church that has disappeared almost completely (de Vaux 1938: 256, 228).

The central mosaic was surrounded by a 0.70 m-wide border (mosaic also), that had representations of various buildings, separated by trees. Originally it had probably 24 monuments. These were evidently churches, each one with a geographical name. Unfortunately only about half have survived. These are: ΝΗΚΩΠΟΛΕΙC, [. . .] ΠΟΛΕΙC, ΑCΚΑΛΟΝ,

ΜΑΗΟΥΜΑC, [ΓΑ]ΖΑ, ΩΔ[ΡΟΑ], [ΧΕΡΑΧΜΟ]ΥΒΑ, ΑΡΕΩΠΟΛΕΙC, ΓΑΔΟΡΟΝ, ΕC[ΒΟΥC], ΒΕΛΕΜΟΥΝΙΜ (de Vaux 1938: 240-241).

A modern wall, built right through the mosaic, has left only the two first letters of the name Εσβους. No traces of the representation of the Εσβους church are left.

The mosaic was restored (probably after the iconoclasts did their work), at the beginning of the 8th century (de Vaux 1938: 239-240).[121]

The discovery of the mosaic of Ma'in began a scholarly dispute about the ecclesiastical divisions in Palestine-Arabia. The presence of Εσβους in a mosaic that has representations of churches belonging mainly to the provinces of Palestine has given rise to the question whether Εσβους was a part of *Palaestina III* or of Arabia in the 7th century, and so, if it was under the patriarch of Jerusalem or of Antioch.[122] There is also the question whether the province of Arabia was still under Antioch or had been transferred to the Jerusalem patriarchate. But the mosaic is too fragmentary[123] to give us a sure answer.

We now come to the end of an epoch. As summarized by Avi-Yonah (1977: 124), the Byzantine administration in Syria-Palestine "received a serious blow during the Persian conquest of Palestine in 614. Laboriously re-established by Heraclius in 627, it went down permanently as the result of the Arab conquest of 636-640."

References[124]

Abel, F. M.
  1933 *Géographie de la Palestine*, vol. 1. Paris: Gabalda.

  1938 Vol. 2.

Albright, W. F.
  1940 *From the Stone Age to Christianity*. Baltimore: Johns Hopkins.

Alt, A.
  1942 Die letzte Grenzverschiebung zwischen den römischen Provinzen Arabia und Palaestina. *ZDPV* 65: 68-76.

Arrian
  1958 *Anabasis Alexandri*, vol. 1. Trans. E. Iliff Robson, from Greek. Loeb Classical Library. London: Heinemann.

Avi-Yonah, M.
  1954 *The Madaba Mosaic Map*. Jerusalem: Israel Exploration Society.

  1977 *The Holy Land*, rev. ed. Grand Rapids, MI: Baker.

Bartlett, J. R.
1978 The Conquest of Sihon's Kingdom: A Literary Re-Examination. *JBL* 97: 347-351.

Behâ ed-Dîn [Bahā' al-Dīn]
1897 *The Life of Saladin*. Trans. by C. R. Conder from French . Vol. 13 of the library of the Palestine Pilgrims' Text Society. London: Palestine Pilgrims' Text Society.

Benzinger, I.
1907 Esbus. Col. 613 of vol. 11 of *Paulys Real-Encyclopädie der Classischen Altertums-Wissenschaft*, ed. G. Wissowa. Stuttgart: Metzler.

Bietenhard, H.
1977 Die syrische Dekapolis von Pompeius bis Traian. Pp. 220-261 in vol. 8 of *Aufstieg und Niedergang der römischen Welt*, eds. H. Temporini and W. Haase. Berlin: De Gruyter.

Bowersock, G. W.
1971 A Report on Arabia Provincia. *JRS* 61: 219-242.

1973 Syria under Vespasian. *JRS* 63: 133-140.

1976 Limes Arabicus. *Harvard Studies in Classical Philology* 80: 219-229.

Brooke, A. E.; McLean, N.; and Thackeray, H. St. John; eds.
1906- *The Old Testament in Greek*, 2 vols.
1935 London: Cambridge University.

Brown, F.; Driver, S. R.; and Briggs, C. A.; eds.
1907 *A Hebrew and English Lexicon of the Old Testament*. Oxford: Clarendon.

Cheyne, T. K., and Black, J. S., eds.
1901 Heshbon. Col. 2044 in vol. 2 of *Encyclopaedia Biblica*. London: Adam and Charles Black.

Conder, C. R.
1882 Lieutenant Conder's Report No. IX: Heshbon and Its Cromlechs. *PEFQS* 14: 7-15.

1892 *Heth and Moab*. London: Alexander P. Watt.

n.d. *Palestine*. New York: Dodd, Mead.

Diodorus Siculus
1947 *Diodorus of Sicily*, vol. 9. Trans. R. M. Greer, from Greek. Loeb Classical Library. Cambridge: Harvard University.

Egeria [Aetheria]
1970 *Egeria: Diary of a Pilgrimage*. Trans. G. E. Gingras, from Latin. Vol. 38 in *ACW*. New York: Newman.

Eubel, C., *et al.*
1914 *Hierarchia Catholica Medii Aevi*, vol. 2. Regensberg: Libraria Regensbergiana.

Eusebius Pamphili
1857 *Chronicon*. *PG* 19: cols. 99-598.

1866 *Chronicon*. Trans. Jerome, from Greek into Latin. *PL* 27: cols. 11-508.

1966 *Das Onomastikon der biblischen Ortsnamen*. Ed. Erich Klostermann. Greek text and Latin trans. Hildesheim (Germany): Olms.

Fortescue, A.
1907 *The Orthodox Eastern Church*. London: Catholic Truth Society.

Gasquet, A., ed.
1926- *Biblia Sacra Iuxta Latinam Vulgatam*, 10
1953 vols. Rome: Typis Polyglottis Vaticanis.

Glueck, N.
1934a Explorations in Eastern Palestine, I. *Annual of the American Schools of Oriental Research* 14: 1-113.

1935 Explorations in Eastern Palestine, II. *Annual of the American Schools of Oriental Research* 15: 1-202.

1951 Explorations in Eastern Palestine, IV. Part 1: text. *Annual of the American Schools of Oriental Research* 25-28: 1-423.

Goldstein, J. A.
1975 The Tales of the Tobiads. Pp. 85-123 in vol. 3 of *Studies for Morton Smith at Sixty*. Leiden: Brill.

1976 *I Maccabees: A New Translation with Introduction and Commentary*. Vol. 41 of the *AB*. Garden City, NY: Doubleday.

Heidet, L.
1903 Hésébon. Cols. 657-663 in vol. 3 of *Dictionnaire de la Bible*, ed. F. G. Vigouroux. Paris: Letouzey et Ané.

Herodotus
1889 *History*. Trans. G. Rawlinson, from Greek. New York: Appleton.

Hill, G. F.
1922 *Catalogue of the Greek Coins of Arabia, Mesopotamia and Persia*. London: British Museum.

Horn, S. H.
1960 *Seventh-day Adventist Bible Dictionary*. Washington: Review and Herald.

Hotzelt, W.
1943 Die kirchliche Organisation Palästinas im 7. Jahrhundert. *ZDPV* 66: 72-84.

James, E. G.
1954 Hešbon. Pp. 1062-1063 in vol. 1 of *Dictionary of Greek and Roman Geography*, ed. W. Smith. Boston: Little, Brown.

Jones, A. H. M.
1971 *The Cities of the Eastern Roman Provinces*, 2nd rev. ed. Oxford: Clarendon.

Josephus, Flavius
1926- *Josephus*, 9 vols. Trans. H. St. J.
1965 Thackeray *et al.* Loeb Classical Library. London: Heinemann.

Koehler, L., and Baumgartner, W.
1958 *Lexicon in Veteris Testamenti Libros.* Leiden: Brill.

Kraeling, E. G. H.
1956 *Rand McNally Bible Atlas.* Chicago: Rand McNally.

Lapp, P. W.
1976 'Iraq el-Emir. Pp. 527-531 in vol. 2 of *Encyclopedia of Archaeological Excavations in the Holy Land*, ed. M. Avi-Yonah. Englewood Cliffs, NJ: Prentice-Hall.

Lifshitz, B.
1969 Légions romaines en Palestine. Pp. 458-469 in vol. 102 of *Collection Latomus.* Bruxelles: Latomus.

Lombardi, G.
1963 Hešbōn. Col. 1214 in vol. 3 of *Enciclopedia de la Biblia*, eds. A. Diez-Macho and S. Bartina. Barcelona: Garriga.

McCown, C. C.
1957 The 'Iraq el-Emir and the Tobiads. *BA* 20: 63-76.

Mansi, J. D., ed.
1960a *Sacrorum Conciliorum Nova et Amplissima Collectio*, vol. 2. Graz (Austria): Akademische Druck-Verlagsanstalt.

1960b Vol. 4.

1960c Vol. 7.

1960d Vol. 10.

Mazar, B.
1957 The Tobiads. *IEJ* 7: 137-145, 229-238.

Merrill, S.
1881 *East of the Jordan.* London: Bentley.

Mittmann, S.
1970 *Beiträge zur Siedlungs- und Territorialgeschichte des nördlichen Ostjordanlandes.* Wiesbaden: Harrassowitz.

Mukadassi
1892 *Description of Syria, Including Palestine.* Trans. G. Le Strange, from Arabic. Vol. 3, no. 3 of the library of the Palestine Pilgrims' Text Society. London: Palestine Pilgrims' Text Society.

Negev, A.
1977 The Nabateans and the Provincia Arabia. Pp. 520-686 in vol. 8 of *Aufstieg und Niedergang der römischen Welt*, eds. H. Temporini and W. Haase. Berlin: De Gruyter.

Newton, A. P., ed.
1926 *Travel and Travellers of the Middle Ages.* New York: Knopf.

Nichol, F. D., ed.
1953 *The Seventh-day Adventist Bible Commentary*, vol. 1. Washington: Review and Herald.

1954a Vol. 2.

1954b Vol. 3.

1955 Vol. 4.

Notitia Dignitatum [Register of Dignitaries]
1899 Vol. 6, no. 4 in *Translations and Reprints from Original Sources of European History.* Philadelphia: University of Pennsylvania.

Parker, S. T.
1975 The Decapolis Reviewed. *JBL* 94: 437-441.

Parkes, J.
1949 *A History of Palestine from 135 A.D. to Modern Times.* New York: Oxford University.

Peake, F. G.
1958 *A History of Jordan and Its Tribes.* Coral Gables, FL: University of Miami.

PG
1857 *Patrologiae Cursus Completus. Series Graeca*, vol. 19, ed. J.-P. Migne. Paris: Migne.

1879 Vol. 137.

Philo Judaeus
1929 *Philo*, vol. 1. Trans. F. H. Colson and G. H. Whitaker, from Greek. Loeb Classical Library. London: Heinemann.

PL
1850 *Patrologiae Cursus Completus.* Series Latina, vol. 82, ed. J.-P. Migne. Paris: Migne.

1855 Vol. 201.

1866 Vol. 27.

Plinius Secundus, C.
1961 *Natural History*, vol. 2. Trans. H. Rackam, from Latin. Loeb Classical Library. Cambridge, MA: Harvard University.

Post, G. A.
1888 Narrative of a Scientific Expedition in the Trans-Jordanic Region in the Spring of 1886. *PEFQS* 20: 175-237.

Pritchard, J. B., ed.
1950 *Ancient Near Eastern Texts Relating to the Old Testament.* Princeton: Princeton University.

Ptolemaus, C.
1966 *Geographia.* Trans. from Greek into Latin. Amsterdam: Theatrum Orbis Terrarum.

Rahlfs, A., ed.
1949 *Septuaginta id est Vetus Testamentum Graece Iuxta LXX Interpretes*, 2 vols. Stuttgart: Privilegierte Württembergische Bibelanstalt.

Salaville, S.
1910 Hesebon. P. 298 in vol. 7 of *The Catholic Encyclopedia*, ed. C. G. Herbermann *et al.* New York: Appleton.

Saller, S. J.
1941a *The Memorial of Moses on Mount Nebo*, vol. 1. Jerusalem: Franciscan.

1941b Vol. 2.

Saller, S. J., and Bagatti, B.
1949 *The Town of Nebo.* Jerusalem: Franciscan.

Sanuto, M.
1896 *Secrets for True Crusaders to Help Them to Recover the Holy Land.* Trans. A. Stewart, from Latin. Vol. 12, No. 2 of the library of the Palestine Pilgrims' Text Society. London: Palestine Pilgrims' Text Society.

Saulcy, F. de
1865 *Voyage en Terre Sainte*, vol. I. Paris: Didier.

Schaff, P., and Wace, H., eds.
1900 *A Select Library of Nicene and Post-Nicene Fathers of the Christian Church*, 2nd series, vol. 14. New York: Scribner.

Schürer, E.
n.d. *A History of the Jewish People in the Time of Jesus Christ.* 5 vols. New York: Scribner.

Seetzen, U. J.
1854 *Reisen duch Syrien, Palästina, Phönicien, die Transjordan-Länder, Arabia Petraea und Unter-Aegypten*, vol. 1. Berlin: Reimer.

Simons, J.
1959 *The Geographical and Topographical Texts of the Old Testament.* Leiden: Brill.

Smith, G. A.
1902 *The Historical Geography of the Holy Land.* London: Hodder and Stoughton.

Speidel, M. P.
1977 The Roman Army in Arabia. Pp. 687-730 in vol. 8 of *Aufstieg und Niedergang der röm ischen Welt*, eds. H. Temporini and W. Haase. Berlin: De Gruyter.

Stein, A.
1940 Surveys on the Roman Frontier in Iraq and Transjordan. *Geographical Journal* 95: 428-439.

Swete, H. B.
1902 *An Introduction to the Old Testament in Greek.* Cambridge: University.

Thomas, D. W., ed.
1965 *Documents From Old Testament Times.* New York: Harper.

Thomsen, P.
1917 Die römischen Meilensteine der Provinzen Syria, Arabia und Palaestina. *ZDPV* 40: 1-141.

Thomson, W. M.
1885 *The Land and the Book.* New York: Harper.

Tobler, T.
1867 *Bibliographia Geographica Palaestinae.* Leipzig: Hirzel.

Van Zyl, A. H.
1960 *The Moabites.* Leiden: Brill.

Vaux, R. de
1938 Chronique. *RB* 47: 227-258.

Will, E.
1977 L'édifice dit Qasr el Abd à Araq al Amir (Jordanie). *Comptes rendus de l'Academie des Inscriptions et Belles-Lettres*, 69-85.

Wright, G. E., and Filson, F. V., eds.
1956   *The Westminster Historical Atlas to the Bible*. Philadelphia: Westminster.

Additional Resource Material

Arnold, T. W.
1927   Muslim Civilization During the Abbasid Period. Pp. 274-299 in vol. 4 of *The Cambridge Medieval History*, ed. H. M. Gwatkin *et al*. New York: Macmillan.

Baly, D.
1957   *The Geography of the Bible*. New York: Harper.

Barnes, T. D.
1975   The Unity of the Verona List. *Zeitschrift für Papyrologie und Epigraphik* 16: 275-279.

Becker, C. H.
1913   The Expansion of the Saracens. Pp. 329-364 in vol. 2 of *The Cambridge Medieval History*, ed. H. M. Gwatkin *et al*. New York: Macmillan.

Burchard of Mount Sion
1896   *Description of the Holy Land*. Trans. A. Stewart, from Latin. Vol. 12, No. 1 of the Library of the Palestine Pilgrims' Text Society. London: Palestine Pilgrims' Text Society.

Eubel, C., *et al*.
1913   *Hierarchia Catholica Medii Aevi*, vol. 1. Regensberg: Libraria Regensbergiana.

Fabri, F.
1892   *The Book of the Wanderings of Brother Felix Fabri*, vol. 1, part 1. Trans. A. Stewart, from Latin. Vol. 7 of the library of the Palestine Pilgrims' Text Society. London: Palestine Pilgrims' Text Society.

1893   Vol. 2, part 2. Vol. 10 of the library of the Palestine Pilgrims' Text Society.

Faris, N. A., ed.
1964   *The Arab Heritage*. Princeton, NJ: Princeton University.

Glueck, N.
1934b Explorations in Eastern Palestine and the Negev. *Bulletin of the American Schools of Oriental Research* 55: 3-21.

1940   *The Other Side of the Jordan*. New Haven, CT: American Schools of Oriental Research.

Hefele, K. J. von
1896   *A History of the Councils of the Church From the Original Documents*, vol. 5. Trans. W. R. Clark, from German. Edinburgh: T. and T. Clark.

Hitti, P. I.
1957   *History of Syria Including Lebanon and Palestine*. London: Macmillan.

1961   *The Near East in History*. Princeton, NJ: Van Nostrand.

Kidd, B. J.
1927   *The Churches of Eastern Christendom From A.D. 451 to the Present Time*. London: Faith Press.

Krüeger, G.
1963   Monothelites. Pp. 480-484 in vol. 7 of *The New Schaff-Herzog Encyclopedia of Religious Knowledge*, ed. S. M. Jackson. Grand Rapids, MI: Baker.

McClintock, J., and Strong, J., eds.
1894   Heshbon. P. 220 in vol. 4 of *Cyclopaedia of Biblical, Theological, and Ecclesiastical Literature*. New York: Harper.

Poloner, J.
1894   *Description of the Holy Land*. Trans. A. Stewart, from Latin. Vol. 6, no. 4 of the library of the Palestine Pilgrims' Text Society. London: Palestine Pilgrims' Text Society.

Rostovtzeff, M. I.
1941   *The Social and Economic History of the Hellenistic World*. Oxford: Clarendon.

Rowley, H. H.
1961   *The Modern Reader's Bible Atlas*. New York: Association.

Strabo
1916   *The Geography of Strabo*, vol. 1. Trans H. L. Jones, from Greek. Loeb Classical Library. London: Heinemann.

Theoderich
1891   *Theoderich's Description of the Holy Places*. Trans. A. Stewart. Vol. 5, no. 4 of the library of the Palestine Pilgrims' Text Society. London: Palestine Pilgrims' Text Society.

Vitry, J. de
1897   *The History of Jerusalem*. Trans. A. Stewart, from Latin. Vol. 11, no. 2 of the library of the Palestine Pilgrims' Text Society. London: Palestine Pilgrims' Text Society.

Endnotes

[1]The "Balkâ District" is already mentioned by Mukadassi (born A.D. 946; 1892: 56). F. M. Abel (1933: 383) considers King Balak of Moses' time as *"le héros éponyme de la province de Belqa."*

[2]See also J. Simons (1959: 36-38, 128, 131); E. G. H. Kraeling (1956: 225, map 1) extends it, mistakenly, from the Arnon to the Zered (*Wâdi el-Hesâ*). This Belqa should not be mistaken for the *sanjak* of *Balqā*, one of the administrative divisions of the *pashalik* of Beirut, that included Samaria, after the administrative reorganization made by Sultan Abdul Hamid II (1876-1909). See James Parkes (1949: 221).

[3]U. J. Seetzen, who was the first Western visitor to Heshbon in the 19th century (1806), remarks: "the open, rolling and hilly environment here became almost an unending plain" (1854: 407). See Josh 13:9, 16, 17, 21.

[4] See in Num 33:44 the name בעיי העברים.

[5]*Cf.* Josephus (*Ant.* 4.8.48): επι τω ορει τω 'Αβαρει; Eusebius (1966: 16): 'Αβαρειμ (Deut 32, 49). ορος εν ω Μωυσης τελευτα. λεγεται δε ειναι "ορος Ναβαυ ο 'εστιν εν γ η Μωαβ 'αντικρυ 'Ιεριχω." . . .

[6]See also Num 25.

[7]Here is where the Israelites camped "and the people began to commit whoredom with the daughters of Moab" (Num 25:1).

[8]This map is copied from Saller and Bagatti (1949: facing p. 1).

[9]George A. Post, who visited Hesban and camped "by the stream that flows from 'Ain Hesbân," found the water "cool and clear, and very abundant" (1888: 191).

[10]It flows past Livias, called now *Tell el-Râmeh*. See Nelson Glueck (1951: 389, 394).

[11]See about the thermal waters of Baaras in Josephus *JW* 7.6.3, *cf.* Abel 1933: 460-461.

[12]Abel (1933: 68) gives the altitude as 874 m. Mount Nebo, 8 km to the southwest, is considerably lower: 835 m (Abel 1933: 63, 379).

[13]Letter of Awni Dajani, Director of the Department of Antiquities of the Hashemite Kingdom of Jordan, to W. Vyhmeister, of December 12, 1966, from Amman.

[14]Several variants are found that appear in cursive MSS of the LXX. A sample of these variants is given here with the symbols used by Brooke, McLean, and Thackeray and their numbers and dates (centuries in Roman numerals) taken from Swete (1902: 148-154): εσσεβων, b (19, X?), kᵃ (58, XIII), m (72, XIII); εσσσεβων, g (54, XIII-XIV), f (53, A.D. 1439), n (75, A.D. 1126); εβων, q (120, XI); εσεβεις, Philo, all his codices (thus far these are all variant readings in Num 21:27); εσεων, f; εσβων, xˣ (London, British Museum, Curzon 66); ασεβων, o (82, XII); ευσεβων, w (Athens, bibl. Nat. 44, XIII); εσεβοβ, u (Jerusalem, Holy Sepulchre, 2, IX).

[15]As claimed by Heidet (1903: col. 657).

[16]κασφω in the Codex Sinaiticus. See Rahlfs (1949), 1 Macc 5:26 (apparatus).

[17]'Εσεβων, 'ερμηνευεται λογιομοι. ουτοι δεισιν αινιγματα ασαφειας γεμοντα. Philo. Legum Allegoria 3.80. *Cf.* 3.233 where the name is interpreted as τα αινιγματα τα σοφιστικα.

[18]Alternative spelling Σεβωνιτιν. See also *Ant.* 15.8.5.

[19]These last three forms are, respectively, accusative, dative and genitive case forms of the district's name.

[20]The Latin transliteration appears here as *Esbuta*.

[21]According to Hill some coins have been attributed to Caracalla (211-217).

[22]Milestones No. 299, inscriptions *c* and *d* and No. 230, inscription *b*.

[23]Milestone No. 230, inscription *c*.

[24]Margin, *Esbundon*.

[25]Variant ιεβους, in V (cod. Vaticanus gr. 1456).

[26]Variant *Esbon*, in A (cod. Sangallensis 133), and B (cod. Berolinensis theol. Lat. 353).

[27]Variant εσεβουν, in V.

[28]Variant ιεβους, in Vallarsi.

[29]Variant ιεβους, in V.

[30]Variant εσεβων, in V.

[31]Many variant spellings are given, though, in Gasquet (1926-1953). We are going to transcribe one of each, with the symbol of the MS where that spelling appears, and the manuscript's date (century) in parentheses (as given by Gasquet): *ebon*, and *sebon*, O (7th-8th); *esbon*, A (7th-8th); *essebon*, and *elssebon*, S (8th); *iessebon*, S² (8th); *hesebon*, *et sebon*, and *et hesaba et hesebon*, C

(8th-9th); *esebon*, Φ^V2 (9th); *esaebon* Φ^P2 (9th); *saebon*, Φ^P* (9th); *hesbon*, Θ (9th); *aesebon*, P⁴ (9th); *ebeson*, Σ^T (10th); *esehon*, Σ^O* (12th); *esebom*, Λ^H (12th); and *osebon*, Ψ^B (12th).

[32]The spelling *Exebon*, as Egeria's translator points out (194), is not found anywhere else.

[33]Margin, Εισβουντος.The Latin version of his name is *Zosys* (margin, *Zosius*) *Isbuntis*. Mansi 1960b: cols. 1269 [Greek], 1270 [Latin].

[34]In Latin, *Zosio civitatis Esbuntorum* (with variant spellings in different MSS: Corb., *Ebuntorum*; Paris. *Erbuntorum*; Divion. *Subontrorum*). Mansi 1960c: cols. 167 [Latin], 168 [Greek].

[35]See de Vaux 1938: 254.

[36]The picture has been copied from Saller 1941b: pl. 42.2.

[37]See also Salaville 1910: 298.

[38]In the Greek version is Θεοδωρω επισκωπω Εσβουντων. Mansi 1960d: cols. 815 [Latin], 816 [Greek].

[39]The Greek Translation (col. 813) has 'Εσβουντων.

[40]Fritz Steppat, director of the "Orient-Institut der Deutschen Morgenländischen Gesellschaft" in Beirut, in letter to W. Vyhmeister of January 2, 1967, gives the name as *Gabal Husbân*, and refers to Tabari's work (ed. de Goeje) 1: 509. Andrew Bowling, of Haigazian College, Beirut, in letter to W. Vyhmeister of March, 1967, makes reference to the *Encyclopedia of Islam*.

[41]The transliteration given here is really *Hesbân*, but it is based on the same Arabic form as *Hesbân*.

[42]Tobler gives the title of ha-Parchi's work as *On the Geography of Palestine: From Jewish Sources.*

[43]Abu el-Fida, *Tabula Syriae*, p. 11, mentioned by James (1954: 1063). James gives the spelling *Chosban*. But the preferred vocalization is *Husbân*, according to Steppat (1967). See Tobler 1867: 34.

[44]Their reports appear in Appendix B.

[45]Lawrence T. Geraty "Heshbon in the Bible, Literary Sources, and Archaeology". Paper presented at the Heshbon Symposium of the Society of Biblical Literature, on December 29, 1977. San Francisco, California. *Cf.* pp. 10-12.

[46]The chronological information given in this chapter is largely based on Horn (1960).

[47]Identified with *Tell ᶜAshtarah*, 33 km. east of the Lake of Galilee. See Horn (1960: 84).

[48]The validity of this statement has more recently been called into question by a number of scholars based on the data turned up by new surface surveys finding Late Bronze Age remains in Transjordan at least as far south as Moab.

[49]See also Conder (1882: 7-15).

[50]*Cf.* Albright 1940: 95-96, who favors the Neolithic Period.

[51]He had also subjugated certain Midianite princes, five of whom are mentioned in Josh 13:21 as defeated also by Moses.

[52]Num 22:1; 31:12; 33:48; 36:13. See also Num 25. The possibility has been suggested that the name originated during the Moabite occupation of this region during the time of the Judges (Judg 3:12-30). See Van Zyl (1960: 115). But this explanation seems hardly necessary since it is clear that the Moabites occupied the territory north of the Arnon before Sihon's conquests. See also (c) and (d).

[53]The "song of mockery" is the one in Num 21:27-30.

[54]See next section in this chapter.

[55]The Ammonite king's claim in Judg 11:13 has to be understood as referring to the combined territories of Ammonites and Moabites at that time (*ca.* 1100 B.C.). *Cf.* Judg 11:24.

[56]Bartlett (1970: 261) considers, without clear biblical support, as "most probable" that Sihon's kingdom was confined to the "the plain' (המישר), the table-land stretching southward from Heshbon to the *wâdi eth-thamad.* . . ."

[57]Even Mesha, king of Moab, in the "Moabite Stone," claims that the "men of Gad had long dwelt in the land of Ataroth" (Thomas 1965: 196).

[58]*Cf.* 1 Chr 6:81. De Saulcy (1865: 287) mistakenly contends that the name Gad, in Josh 21:38, 39 applies only to Ramoth of Gilead and Mahanaim.

[59]Assuming that he is the original author of Cant 7:4.

[60]In Appendix B, the meaning attributed to this expression by several authors will be mentioned.

[61]*Cf.* the Moabite Stone, Thomas (1965: 196).

[62]Van Zyl understands that the מישור of 2 Chr 26:10 is the table-land between Arnon and Heshbon. It is true that מישור is often used to designate this region (cf. Deut 3:10; 4:43; Josh 13:9, 16, 17, 21; 20:8; Jer 48:8, 21). But the context would seem to require here plains in southern Judah. Simons (1959: 63-64) says that "it is not impossible that in 2 Ch. xxvi 10 'the M.' refers to cisjordan Sharon" (cf. also Nichol 1954b: 283). It is not possible to insist that Mishor is always a proper noun. Compare its use in Jer 21:13 (Simons 1959: 444). On the other hand, based only on this key word, it cannot be said that Van Zyl is wrong.

[63]Salchad? See Simons (1959: 122).

[64]Or, "on all the pasture-lands of Sharon" (Simons 1959: 123).

[65]By "a century before" is meant a century before the events discussed here.

[66]Salamanu appears, together with Jehoahaz of Judah, in an inscription of Tiglath-pileser III found in Nimrud (Thomas 1965: 56).

[67]Identified with Irbid, in the ʿAjlûn, but only as a "tentative suggestion," by Simons (1959: 464).

[68]Assyrian royal inscriptions and Jer 48 testify to the fact that in the second half of the 7th century B.C. Moab still possessed the region north of the Arnon (Van Zyl 1960: 154).

[69]With the title of šarru in Assyrian inscriptions (Van Zyl 1960: 151).

[70]Waterman, Royal Correspondence, 1: 440, as cited by Van Zyl (1960: 153).

[71]The dates apply to chapters 46-51.

[72]Milkom, in Hebrew (Jer 49:3), could refer to the Ammonites' main god (cf. 1 Kgs 11:5, 33; 2 Kgs 23:13).

[73]As already pointed out, Heshbon's name was spelled in various ways during the Hellenistic, Maccabean, Roman, and Byzantine periods. To avoid any confusion, only one of these spellings will be used throughout this section: namely, Esbus, one of the spellings given by Eusebius, in its Latin transliteration as given by his translator, Jerome.

[74]Arrian (Anab. Alex 3.1) says: και Φοινικιαν τε και Συριαν και της ᾿Αραβιας τα πολλα υπο ᾿Αλεξανδρου εχομενα. It is still debated what "all of Arabia" meant. But it probably included at least what had once been a part of the Persian Empire. See Abel (1938: 125).

[75]Throughout this section I am heavily indebted to Avi-Yonah and also to a considerable extent to Abel. A number of other references, to both primary and secondary sources, will be given in the endnotes throughout this section. In addition, mention may be made here of several works which may be of general interest to the reader because, even though not dealing only with our specific subject area as such, they shed light on aspects of the historical geography of portions of Transjordan for one or more of the periods with which we are concerned: G. W. Bowersock (1971: 219); A. H. M. Jones (1971); S. Mittmann (1970); F. G. Peake (1958); and A. Stein (1940: 428-439).

[76]Cf. Jones (1971: 239-240, 449-450) who suggests that district names ending in "...itis" originated in Ptolemaic times. This ending is, of course, common in the names of Egyptian nomes.

[77]P. Zen. 59003, 59005, 59075, 59076.

[78]Mazar 1957: 139. (P. Zen. 59075-59076).

[79]That is, a colony of soldiers of various nationalities. Mazar 1957: 139. (P. Zen. 59003).

[80]Mazar 1957: 140. (P. Lond. Inv. 2358).

[81]Mazar 1957: 140. (P. Zen. 59003).

[82]See also Will (1977: 69-85), Lapp (1976: 527-531), and Goldstein (1975: 85-123; 1976: 298-299).

[83]The term used is ᾿Εσσεβωνιτιδος.

[84]In the years 276-272, 260-255, 246-241, and 221-217. See Avi-Yonah (1977: 42).

[85]Cf. 2 Macc 3:5; 4:4; 8:8. Six of the governors of "Coelesyria and Phoenicia" as known from the sources were Ptolemy, son of Thraseas (time of Antiochus III), Apollonius, son of Thraseas, and Apollonius, son of Mnestheus (under Seleucus IV), Seron and Ptolemy (under Antiochus IV), and Apollonius (appointed by Demetrius II). Avi-Yonah (1977: 44, 45).

[86]1 Macc 5:25; 9:35-42; Josephus Ant. 13.1.2. See Abel (1938: 136-137).

[87]See Josephus Ant. 13.13.5; 13.15.2-4; Wars 1.4.4. Cf. E. Schürer [n.d.], First Div., 2: 351-352.

[88]Cf. Josephus, Ant. 13.16.3; Wars 1.5.3.

[89]According to Josephus, Ant. 14.1.4, these were: Madaba, Naballo, Libyas, Tharabasa, Agala, Athone, Zoar, Orone, Marissa, Rudda, Lussa, and Oruba.

[90]In a rather arbitrary way, "Roman times" will stand here for the period that starts with Pompey's capture of Jerusalem in 63 B.C. and ends with the establishment of Constantinople as a second capital of the Roman empire in A.D. 330.

[91]See also Bietenhard (1977: 220-261), Parker (1975: 437-441), and Negev (1977: 520-686).

[92]L. Mitchel's report on the Hellenistic and Roman remains at Tell Hesban can be found in Hesban 7.

[93]Cf. Josephus, Ant. 15.7.9. Each division was probably called meris (see Avi-Yonah 1977: 98).

[94]Schürer (First Div. 1: 436-437) thinks, though, that Herod rebuilt "Esbon in Perea." The Greek text reads: συνεκτισεν επι τη Γαλιλαια Γοβα καλουμενον, και, τη Περαια την ᾿Εσεβωνιτιν. The key word here is συνεκτισεν, clearly based on κτιζω. Κτιζω can mean: "To people (a country)," "to build houses and cities (in it)," "to found, to build (a city)," etc.

[95]Schürer (First Div. 2: 355) gives the regnal years of Μαλχος or Μαλιχος as 50-28 B.C.

[96]Josephus (Wars 3.3.3): On "the south it is bounded by the land of Moab, on the east by Arabia, Heshbonitis, Philadelphia, and Gerasa." Cf. Ant. 15.8.5, where Esbus is part of Peraea under Herod the Great.

[97]So Schürer contends (Second Div. 1: 129).

[98]See my further discussion in the next paragraph.

[99]Also sacked were important cities like Philadelphia, Gerasa, Pella, and Scythopolis. Josephus (Wars 2.18.1).

[100]Abel gives as his sources Dio Cassius 68.14, and Ammian 14.8.13; he also points out that Trajan coins have the inscription Arabia adquisita. Bowersock (1971: 231-232) argues persuasively that Bostra, and not Petra, was the capital. For the legion and related military matters see Speidel (1977: 687-730).

[101]The text of the inscriptions is given here as it appears, with comments and bibliographical notes, in Thomsen (1917: 67-68):

"229.[mp V von Esbus, wo der Weg von Mādeba sich mit der Rstr vereinigt] Zehn Mst, vier Inschriften:

"a) '[Imp(eratori) Caes(ari) M(arco) Aur(elio) Antonino p(io) f(elici) Aug(usto) diui magni fil(io) diui [S]eueri nep(oti) [pont(ifici) m]ax(imo) trib(uniciae) p[ot(estatis) co(n)s(uli) II] pro[co(n)s(uli) μιλια E.' CIL III 14 151. GERMER-DURAND: RB 4 (1895) S.398; 5 (1896) S.614. Vgl. Nr. 119a Jahr 219 n. Chr.

"b) '[... et Imperatori Caesari Gal(erio) Ua]ler[io Maximi]ano [pio felici inuicto August]o [m]il(ia) p(assuum) V' = Nr.116a₂. CIL III 14 152. GERMER-DURAND a.a.O.S. 399. Jahr 307 n. Chr.

"c) '... io ... ei ... s no ... aiitio ... Caesari ... i ... in ... απο ᾿Εσβουντος μ(ιλια) [E].' CIL 14 152₁. GERMER-DURAND a.a.O.S.399; 614: '... no ... no ... Ualent ... Caes(ari) nob[ilis]simo inuictisque Caesari[bus] ...n... απο ᾿Εσβουντος μ(ιλια) E.' Jahr 364-375 n. Chr.?

"d) '... tribun(iciae) pot e st(atis) co (n)s(ul) proco(n)s(ul) απο ᾿Εσβουντος [μ(ιλια)] E.' CIL III 14 153. GERMER-DURAND a.a.O.S. 399; 614. Jahr 219 n. Chr.?

"230. [mp VI] Kurz vor dem Abstiege in die Jordan-ebene zwei Mst. drei Inschriften:

"a) = Nr.78b, aber am Schlusse: 'pronepotes ... ref[ecerunt] ... XI.' CIL III 14 154 (zwischen 'Aug(ustus)' und '[p]ont(ifex)' ist hier noch 'pius' zu ergänzen). GERMER-DURAND; RB 6 (1897) S. 591. Jahr 162 n. Chr.

"b) 'Imp(eratori) Caesari G(aio) Iulio Uero Maximino p(io) f(elici) Aug(usto) n(ostro) et G(aio) Iul(io) Uero Maximo nob(ilissimo) Caes(ari) filio Aug(usti) n(ostri) απο ᾿Εσβουντος μ(ιλια) S mil(ia) [p(assuum)] VI.' CIL III 14 154₁. GERMER-DURAND a.a.O.S. 399; 614. Jahr 236 n. Chr.

"c) 'Imperantibus Caesaribus fratribus Caio Ualerio Diocletiano et Mar(co) Aur(elio) Maximiano piis felicibus inuictis Aug(ustis) a Esb(unte) m(ilia) p(assuum) S.' GERMER-DURAND: Rev. august. 1903 S. 432 f. Jahr 288 n. Chr."

[102]Ptolemy (*Geog* 5.16) gives the transitional title to one section of his description: "Syria-Palestine or Judea."

[103]Some of the coins have been dated in the reign of Caracalla (211-217), by Heidet (1903: col. 663); James (1954: 1063); and Benzinger (1907: col. 613) though this is not generally accepted today. See Hill (1922: xxxiii). Besides Esbus, other cities of Arabia that minted their own money were: Edrei, Bostra, Philippopolis, Canatha, Dion, Gerasa, Philadelphia, and Madaba (Abel 1938: 187).

[104]Diocletian divided the empire into four prefectures: Gaul, Italy, Illyricum, and East. The prefecture of the East was divided into three dioceses: Asia, Pontus, and East. Parkes (1949: 57). See also A. Fortescue (1907: 21-22).

[105]Dated between 395-407 by Gibbon, in A.D. 402 by Hodgkin and Bury, etc. See *Notitia Dignitatum* (1899: 3). According to the *Notitia* (1899: 5-6) the prefecture of the East was divided about A.D. 400 into five dioceses: Thracia, Asia, Pontus, East, and Egypt. The diocese of the East, in turn, was divided into fifteen provinces: "Palaestina, Phoenice, Syria, Cilicia, Cyprus, Arabia (also a duke and a military count), Isauria, Palaestina Salutaris, Palaestina Secunda, Phoenice Libani, Euphratensis, Syria Salutaris, Osroena, Mesopotamia, Cilicia Secunda."

Other editions of the *Notitia* are Guido Clemente, *La "Notitia Dignitatum"* (Cagliari: Editrice Sarda Fossataro, 1968); and Otto Seeck, ed., *Notitia Dignitatum* (Berlin: Weidmannos, 1876).

[106]Both authors refer to *Cod. Theod.* VII, 4, 304; XVI, 8, 29.

[107]Hierocles, *Synecdemus*, ed. Burckhardt (Teubner, 1893), 717, 8; 719, 12; Georgius Cyprius, *Descriptio Orbis Romani*, ed. Gelzer (Teubner, 1890); and Mansi, under the respective councils and synods. *Cf.* Avi-Yonah (1977: 121), where reference is made to these items.

[108]Avi-Yonah gives credit to Alt, *Palästina-Jahrbuch* 29 (1933): 67ff.

[109]The Council of Nicaea belongs to the "Roman times," but it has been included in this period in order to avoid introducing an unnatural break in what little is known of the ecclesiastical history of Esbus.

[110]The third patriarchal see at that time (A.D. 325) was Rome. Constantinople later became the patriarchal see of the diocese of Thrace. The bishops of Ephesus in the diocese of Asia and of Cappadocian Caesarea in the diocese of Pontus were considered as primates, but not as patriarchs of their respective dioceses. Fortescue (1907: 21-23).

[111]Margin, *Esbundon*. Mansi (1960a: col. 699).

[112]Jerome translates this phrase as "urbs insignis Arabiae" (Eusebius *Onom* 85: 1-6).

[113]Jerome's Latin spellings are used here.

[114]This could indicate that Iazer was located in, or close to, the border of the two districts.

[115]Military establishments located so as to protect the outer frontiers of the Roman empire. See Avi-Yonah (1977: 118-121); *cf.* several recent articles by Bowersock (1971: 219-242; 1973: 133-140; 1976: 219-229).

[116]Avi-Yonah (1977: 178, map 23) places its western limit in Peraea.

[117]Margin, Εισβουντος. In Latin it appears as *Zosys* [*Zosius*] *Isbuntis* (Mansi 1960b: cols. 1269 [Greek], 1270 [Latin]).

[118]At least the same name (*Zosio*) is given to the bishop *civitatis Esbuntorum* (Mansi 1960c: cols. 167 [Latin], 168 [Greek]).

[119]See also Theodore Balsamon's testimony in "Canones Nicaenae Primae Sanctae et Oecumenicae Synodi" (*PG* 1879: cols. 243, 244, 253, 254). He was patriarch of Antioch (1185/91-1195). He wrongly assumes that already at Nicaea (325) Jerusalem was a patriarchal see with jurisdiction over "provinciis Palaestinae, Arabiae et Phoenices" (col. 243). But commenting on the Council of Chalcedon he assigns to Jerusalem only the three Palestines (cols. 253, 254).

[120]See *supra*, p. 5.

[121]The so-called "great inscription," found at the entrance of the church, bears the date 614 in line 5. "According to the era of Bozrah, generally used in Medeba and Nebo, this would correspond to 719/720" (de Vaux 1938: 239-240).

[122]Alt (1942: 68-76) contends that the mosaic does not prove that Esbus was in Palaestina III. W. Hotzelt (1943: 77-84), while conceding that the churches in the Ma'in mosaic were included there because of their relative importance, and regardless of ecclesiastical divisions (74), states that Bozrah belonged to the patriarchate of Jerusalem from 649 on (77-78, 81). But he bases this last statement on the letters of Pope Martin I (of the year 649) that are far from being conclusive on this matter (see text of the letters in Mansi 1960d: cols. 806-815).

[123]See picture in de Vaux (1938: plate 10).

[124]The abbreviations which appear in this list of references have been taken from the list of abbreviations of books and periodicals published in *Andrews University Seminary Studies* (*AUSS*).

Chapter Two

HESBAN DURING THE ARAB PERIOD:
A.D. 635 TO THE PRESENT

Malcolm B. Russell

Hesban During the Arab Period: A.D. 635 to the Present

Introduction

Longer by far than the preceding cultural epochs, the period of Muslim rule over Husbān[1] witnessed numerous and significant changes in the region's population, religion, means of livelihood, and political allegiance. The Byzantine era of relative prosperity and dense population nevertheless ended only after more than a century of conflict and disorder. Muslim rule, bringing peace and security, began with little change in levels of wealth, despite its redistribution. This was the period of Arab rule by the Orthodox caliphs, and then by the Umayyad dynasty that ruled from Damascus, roughly A.D. 635-750. Several Umayyad caliphs enjoyed Transjordan, and built desert castles there, east of Hesban. Definite decline set in only after 750 with the coming of 'Abbāsid (Abbasid) rule in Iraq, and continued with the local dynasties that ruled geographical Syria after the 9th century. However, beginning with the arrival of the Crusades (1100) and the consequent Muslim unity under the 'Ayyūbids (Ayyubids), there was a brief and unusual reprieve for Transjordan in general, and Hesban in particular, that lasted through much of the Mamlūk (Mamluk) era (1260-1517).

The third period of Muslim rule, that of the Ottoman Turks after 1517, found permanent settlement and formal government at a minimum until the end of the last century. Only the imposition of central authority and the Hashemite emirate after World War I allowed the systematic development of agriculture and an accompanying growth of population. The past 60 years witnessed rapid modernization and social change; the Byzantine standards of wealth and population were regained, then far surpassed.

Well before the Arab conquest of Transjordan, there were strong signs of the decline of Hellenistic culture in the area. Historians generally agree that the inhabitants spoke Aramaic in daily affairs, in contrast to the Greek utilized in ecclesiastical matters. Religiously, the populace tended to subscribe to the heresies; indeed, the last Christian reference to Hesban (then called Esbus) mentions the heretical Monothelism of the Bishop Theodore of Esbus in the mid-7th century (Mansi 1960: cols. 806-815). Well before this, however, much of Transjordan, and specifically the Belqa (the region or district surrounding Hesban), fell within the sphere of the Ghassanid Arab Christian kingdom of the 6th century (Hitti 1957: 403). Their Christianity tempered by Monophysite beliefs, the Ghassanids became particularly important under King al-Hārith V. He worked with the Byzantine emperors to defend the long eastern borders of Greater Syria from raids out of the desert. In this role, the Ghassanid Arabs proved useful though often independent allies of the Byzantines in their struggles with the Persians. Nevertheless, in the early 7th century, the Persian onslaught from the east materialized anyway, destroying many cities and areas of Syria and Palestine. The army of Chosroes Purviz sacked the important town of Madaba, near Hesban, in 613 (Peake 1958: 34). Unless spared by its insignificance, Hesban also likely suffered destruction during these years. One history of Madaba portrays Persian troops marching westwards from Hesban towards Jerusalem (Saba and 'Uzayzi 1961: 114). Although Byzantine control returned to the region, less than 20 years later Arab attacks began in earnest.

The Early Arab Period

The Belqa was located on the edge of the desert and close to the southern limits of Byzantine control, between the Zerqa (Jabbok) and Mujib (Arnon) rivers. Thus it felt almost the first Muslim attacks out of Arabia. The town of Mu'ta, then sometimes considered in the Belqa although south of the Arnon, was attacked in the Prophet Muhammad's lifetime. Orders to invade the region were given in the eleventh year after the Hijra, or 632 (Tabari 1964: 3: 1 > 94). The next year a Muslim force defeated a Byzantine army by Zizya, not far from Hesban, though larger Byzantine forces ousted the Muslims. Undeterred, the Muslim army returned in 634 and Zizya became the base for further attacks (Peake 1958: 50). These first Arab conquests were scattered, Amman holding out until after Damascus was captured (Harding 1960). Hesban probably fell to Arab warriors before their victory at the Yarmuk in 636 that ended Christian rule over Syria.

The few early Muslim historians make no specific mention of Hesban itself. Probably the closest reference is al-Tabari's (839-923) account of Balaam blessing the Children of Israel during the Exodus. This story portrays Balaam as speaking from Jabal or Mt.

Hesban (1964: 509). Nevertheless, administrative accounts and other sources provide a basic outline of life in the early Muslim era. For the first century of Arab rule, under the Umayyads the area flourished, in general. Wealthy Muslims emulated their caliphs and built numerous palaces and fine private houses in the Belqa (Sourdel-Thomine 1960). Several sources mention individuals possessing estates there, which indicate that privately-held land ownership did exist; however, in common with Muslim procedures elsewhere, most agricultural land belonged to the state. Generally it was cultivated by Christian peasants who had remained despite the Arab conquest when the upper and landowning classes fled. Probably the initial impact of the Arab conquest on Hesban was slight. No doubt the church continued to be used for Christian services, rather than being modified as a mosque. Archaeological discoveries from elsewhere show church repairs and other Christian activities in early 8th-century Transjordan.

Administratively, Hesban lay in the midst of the Belqa, with its capital at Amman. In turn, the Belqa formed part of a *jund*, or district, several of them comprising Syria. It appears that the *junds* were occasionally rearranged, for Transjordan towns are included at different times under the *junds* of both Palestine and Damascus (Le Strange 1965: 35-48). Perhaps this was because the Jordan province produced relatively little income, the least in Syria.

Historians and geographers make no reference to Hesban, and take scanty notice of the general Belqa region, after the Abbasids came to power in 750. This is not surprising. At that time, the court, the administration, and the center of intellectual activity shifted to Baghdad and flourished there. Damascus and the rest of Syria became a sometimes restive backwater. Early revolts against the Abbasids spread to the Belqa, but references to specific other events are scanty. Undoubtedly, however, it was then that the vast majority of inhabitants converted to Islam. The Umayyads, strongly Arab in their orientation, had generally discouraged conversions to Islam, for this would reduce the taxation from subject peoples. In contrast, the new caliphs continued to levy discriminatory taxes and other exactions on their Christian subjects and also encouraged their conversion to Islam. (It should be remembered that the *dhimmī*, or protected non-Muslim subject, enjoyed definite rights and freedom from certain liabilities. His treatment in the Arab Muslim empire stood in great contrast with that of contemporary religious minorities in Europe.)

Although the long line of Abbasid caliphs continued in Baghdad until the mid-13th century, administrative and political power increasingly fell into the hands of others after the mid-9th century. A variety of sometimes-competing dynasties ruled Transjordan and the insignificant village of Hesban. Many of these rulers were foreign, non-Arab speaking mercenaries; some were based in Egypt. Among them were the Tulunids, the Fatimids, the Ikhshids, and the Seljuqs. Despite the occasional good administrator, the rulers of these dynasties weakened the economic and military strength of the area, often in battle. Hardly had a number of petty Seljuq dynasties established themselves in Syria than the armies of militant Christians, the Crusaders, marched down the coast, seeking Jerusalem.

The Crusader and Ayyubid Period

After the First Crusade captured most of Palestine from the Muslims in 1099, the East Bank of the Jordan River assumed a geopolitical importance it rarely equaled before or since. The Crusader state cut the natural line of Muslim communications between Syria and Egypt, through Galilee and the Palestinian coast. Instead, communications and trade between Egypt and the East shifted to the Jordanian plateau, descending to Aqaba and thence by water or across the Sinai. It was precisely to cut this route that Pagan the Butler, Lord of Oultrejourdain, fortified al-Kerak; other Crusader fortresses eventually dotted Transjordan.

Hesban, an easily defended height with a spring lying some distance behind it to the north, might be expected to play a part in Muslim attacks on al-Kerak. According to some 19th-century historians, it did, for after one of the unsuccessful thrusts at the Crusader fort, Salāh al-Dīn (Saladin) withdrew his forces to Hesban (Stevenson 1907: 235; Behâ ed-Dîn 1897: 97). However, the logic of the move has not escaped question, largely because of Saladin's subsequent move that allowed the Crusaders to send reinforcements to al-Kerak from Palestine. Saladin may have desired to weaken the Crusaders in Palestine. According to Ibn Jubayr, a contemporary Muslim historian, the Arab armies next attacked Nablus, in northern Palestine (1964: 272). In any case, Saladin's unification of Syria and Egypt, followed by his defeat of the Crusaders at the Battle of Hattin, 1187, ended the Crusader intrusion into most of Palestine. Thereafter, his Ayyubid dynasty governed the area until the establishment of Mamluk rule in the late 1250s.

Hesban at Its Height: The Mamluk Era

Historical evidence overwhelmingly portrays Hesban at its height during the early Mamluk Period. Once again competition between rulers in Egypt and Syria centered on Palestine and provided the East Bank with a strategic and political importance unknown during periods of regional unity. In fact, during the Mamluk Period al-Kerak was a kingdom, often dominated by Egypt or Damascus, perhaps, but nevertheless a political entity in its own right. As a result, foreign resources often flowed into the Transjordan area to garrison its towns, repair the castle at al-Kerak, and maintain members of the royal family who lived there. The historian Maqrīzī gives many instances of this (1837: 1: 141; 1: 205-6).

Although on occasion part of the kingdom of al-Kerak, Hesban generally served as the capital of the southernmost district of Damascus. In this role it flourished. In the 14th century, the Arab geographer and prince Abū al-Fidā' wrote of the town, probably after a visit there. He relates that Hesban was the capital of the Belqa, and indicates other sources of prosperity. It was "a small town, overlooking a valley with trees and mills as well as gardens and fields [or farms]" (1840: 245). Obviously referring to the wadi (valley) west of Hesban, Abū al-Fidā' also noted that it continued to the Ghawr (Ghor), and thus linked Hesban with Jericho. Considering the density of population, the presence of trees tantalizes the historian. Did a moister climate than usual encourage thickets or woods to grow uncultivated in the lower ravines? Recent studies of climatic trends in the Middle East (Brice 1968) unfortunately provide insufficient clues. Alternatively, Abū al-Fidā' may be referring to orchards. If so, this, plus the mention of mills, indicates that capital improvements were relatively secure, and that the conflicts of the early Mamluk Period left the countryside relatively undisturbed. Although scarce today, trees did grace the area somewhat in the 19th century, but since the population was sparse the demand for firewood was small.

Writing a century later, al-Zāhirī again describes Hesban as a place of some importance, claiming that its district comprised some three hundred villages (Ziadeh 1953: 71, 72). Although Nicola Ziadeh, a modern historian of the period, refuses to accept a claim of such magnitude (Ziadeh 1953: 71, 72), in fact the assertion symbolizes the wide area that Hesban ruled. Indeed, in the early 15th century Hesban was evidently the only significant East Bank town between the Yarmuk River and al-Kerak. Thus its towns, though probably fewer than three hundred, nevertheless included all those of the Belqa as well as others to the north. Another indication of the wide use of the town's name is al-Dimashqi's reference to the Nahr al-Zerqa. Often considered the northern limit of the Belqa, al-Dimashqī describes its source as the Hesban area (Le Strange 1965: 110). Other authors mentioning Hesban during the period include Ibn al-Furāt, Qalqashandī, al-'Umarī, and the Jew, ha-Parchi (Heidet 1903: 87-88).

Besides its agricultural and administrative rules, Hesban also served as a rest stop on the postal route from Damascus to al-Kerak. Different authors suggest it was either five or nine days from Damascus (Al-Bakhīt 1976: 14). In any case, as a postal rest stop Hesban no doubt provided the same facilities as those offered travelers on the route to Egypt: a khan to care for animals, an inn for travelers, and a mosque for prayers (Al-Bakhīt 1976: 14).

Another important feature of the town was its defenses. Although they are not described in detail, they must have been substantial, for Yāqūt describes them as "ḥiṣn ḥaṣīn," an invulnerable fortification or stronghold (1965: 3: 859). Presumably certain other facilities existed, such as public baths, but there probably were no hospitals or libraries, and any school would have been small and religious. Although Hesban was never a center of learning, three Arab theologians or legal scholars in the 14th century bore the title "al-Husbānī," thus indicating links with the town. However, the scholars themselves lived in the more important cities of Damascus and Jerusalem (Kahāla n.d.: 1: 164:, 2: 269, 3: 190).

The prosperity of Hesban during the 13th and 14th centuries provides a surprising contrast to the general judgment that Syria and Egypt suffered greatly from Mamluk rapacity and misgovernment. However, Hesban's escape from assault and destruction probably indicates fairly little about conditions in other areas during the period. Indeed, the conclusion that Hesban enjoyed a "golden age" comes primarily from a study of the town, not the wider region. Very probably the town's prominence resulted from the ill-fortunes of larger localities, particularly Amman. This city, intact as late as the mid-13th century, suffered great devastation and ruin by the early 14th, so that Abū al-Fidā' thought its ruins predated Islam (1840: 247). Amman had ruled the Belqa; Hesban became important (though not as large) when it replaced the destroyed city as the capital.

Perhaps the relative insignificance of Hesban helped it avoid some of the disasters that befell Syria and the Belqa during the late Ayyubid and Mamluk periods. Under Kutbugha, in 1260 the Mongols reached al-Kerak, but they may have missed the small town of Hesban on their march south, and thus spared its inhabitants ravages inflicted on Damascus at the end of the century. In an era of mass flights from Syria to Egypt, and from the large cities to the countryside, Hesban suffered comparatively little, and possibly expanded its population as well as its administrative importance.

However, during the rule of the later Mamluks, the town nevertheless suffered from the almost constant internecine warfare that marked the period. Around al-Kerak, various campaigns plundered the gardens to provide forage for their horses (Al-Bakhīt 1976: 34), and at times Hesban must have suffered a similar fate. Because it lay near the border between the kingdoms of Damascus and al-Kerak, the Belqa provided plunder and booty for Mamluk rebels of various kinds. For example, in the 13th century brigands fleeing Egypt laid waste to parts of the region (Maqrīzī 1837: 1: 49). In 1389 the ruler of al-Kerak allied with his royal prisoner, Sultan Barqūq, released him, and together they advanced towards Damascus. Their forces seized the crops of Hesban, as well as the other villages in the Belqa (Ibn Sasra 1963: 40). Whether a similar expedition sacked Hesban and led to its abandonment, the historical materials do not indicate.

Located in a region of mixed farming and herding, perhaps Hesban avoided the famines that occurred during the 14th and 15th centuries. Nevertheless, it would have suffered from the bubonic and pneumonic plagues that spread rapidly—and recurrently—through Syria then. Although sources are scanty about the Belqa, elsewhere in Syria villages became uninhabited as a result of the plague (Ashtor 1976: 302). Al-Bakhīt provides details of numerous natural disasters around al-Kerak (1976: 110-112). Like the effects of the plague in Europe, the results in the Middle East were catastrophic. The population of Syria, estimated at 900,000 during the 13th century by Ashtor (1976: 302) fell precipitously, to 600,000 by the 16th century (Barkan 1958: 20, 27). It had been about four million at the time of the Arab conquest! In contrast to the economic, landholding, and religious effects of the plagues in Europe, in the Middle East the centralist landholding system generally remained unchanged, as did the pattern of production (Dols 1977: 281-283).

In contrast to Dols' generalization about the whole Middle East, given the widespread depopulation of Syria, it was natural for a border zone such as the Belqa to change its method of food production. Whether the survivors of the plague left the area for better-watered lands is unclear; in any case, settled farming and permanent residence became rare. Hesban probably ceased to exist as a town, and the minimum of administration that remained shifted to al-Salt. The East Bank fell under Bedouin rule, and transhumance became the dominant method of producing food. By 1502 the nomads were strong enough to attack al-Kerak and Jerusalem (Muir 1968: 190). Although it was repulsed, the attack itself shows that wide portions of Transjordan had fallen under their control. The charts that show the Ottomans ruling Jordan in succession to the Mamluks are incorrect. The area fell first to the Bedouin.

The Ottoman Period: 1516-1918

In contrast to the rapid crumbling of Mamluk defenses in Syria and Egypt before the Ottoman forces, Transjordan came under Ottoman rule very slowly. In late 1516 the new governor of Damascus, Sībay, headed a detachment of troops that marched to southern Jordan, to fight the Bedouin around al-Kerak and al-Shawbak. Unsuccessful in this attempt to establish order and Ottoman sovereignty, Sībay attempted another mission of pacification and conquest within the next year (Ibn Tūlūn 1952: 120, 124). Apparently a Mamluk, named Gugaiman or Jughayman, led Bedouin resistance to Ottoman rule, and although occasionally caravans travelled again by 1520, Jughayman led later uprisings and avoided defeat until 1529 (Bakhit 1972: 25-26). Even thereafter, Ottoman rule over Transjordan remained an uncertain matter. In 1556, Bedouin insurrections spread throughout the area and spilled over into Palestine and the *sanjak* (province) of Damascus. Once this outbreak was repressed, and an Ottoman fortress ordered at 'Ajlun, tribes in the Belqa attacked farmlands around al-Salt, devastating the fields and plundering the villages for grains. A decade later the governor of al-Kerak was killed by Bedouin (Bakhit 1972: 261, 268).

Eventually, the Ottoman government established a series of fortresses east of the Jordan, parallel to the pilgrim route from Damascus to Medina and Mecca. The main forts were established at 'Ajlūn, al-Salt, al-Kerak, and al-Shawbak. Sultan Sulaymān also ordered additional forts on the pilgrim route itself, at Qatrana, Ma'an, Dhat Haj, and Tabuk. According to Bakhit, the total number of garrison troops was small, running between 50 and 80 officers and men per fortress. Not surprisingly, disorders continued (1972: 105). In both the 17th and 18th centuries, the governors of Damascus had to fight their way into al-Kerak, execute rebellious notables, and reestablish order (Ibn Tūlūn 1952: 219, 321). Located well south of most of Jordan, al-Kerak probably felt less governmental control than other areas, but one governor's account gives ample description of the difficulties of ruling the country. No crops were cultivated, Qansuh al-Ghazzāwi reported in 1571, and the inhabitants remained in a state of rebellion. Because of the mobility of the populace, it was impossible to provision officials and maintain them with the Bedouin (Bakhit 1972: 250-251). A man of some experience in the area, Qansuh had previously served in the honorable position of Amīr al-Hāj (leader of the pilgrimage to the Hijāz [Hijaz]). Perhaps because of his knowledge of the countryside, he was reappointed to that position in 1572, after his report.

Given the circumstances, Ottoman record-keeping was naturally brief, and few Arab geographers or historians passed through the area. Evidently such sources as remain do not even identify the inhabitants of the Belqa during the 16th and 17th centuries (Bakhit 1972: 226). However, the Banu Sakhr (Beni Sakhr), an important tribe who now live in the desert east of Hesban, then owned four farms in the Jordan Valley near Baysan. The inhabitants of the Belqa may have been mostly the Jahāwisha and the Da'jah (Bakhit 1972: 226). For tax purposes, Hesban was a farm, and the Ottoman financial records recorded it as such (Bakhit 1978 interview). Such evidence, however, need not imply the presence of a permanent farming community, for any cultivation was seasonal and probably the work of seminomads living in tents.

The Ottoman sultans valued control over the Transjordanian plateau for two distinct reasons. It provided a buffer against raids from the desert on the much richer and more heavily populated lands of Palestine to the west. Secondly, to the east of Hesban, and parallel to the Jordan Valley, ran the route of the annual Hāj, or pilgrimage, to the sacred cities of the Hijaz. Despite these important Ottoman interests, and the weak Ottoman garrisons, raiders crossed into Palestine frequently. Likewise, the success of the pilgrim convoy oftentimes depended on the leadership—and sometimes largess—of the Amīr al-Hāj. As often as not, he bought off tribes from attacking it, rather than subjecting them by force of arms (among others, see Rafeq 1970: 341 and Bakhit 1972).

Rebellions by local officials or notables often interrupted even nominal Ottoman suzerainty over the East Bank. However, from 1831 to 1840 Syria was occupied by the armies of Muhammad 'Alī, ruler of Egypt. Quickly his troops curbed the Bedouin tribes, but like the Ottomans, he could not retain permanent control of the rural areas east of the Jordan (Ma'oz 1968: 14). Although Egyptians garrisoned al-Kerak and such towns as existed, much of the countryside continued its habitual practices, and probably provided haven for those seeking refuge from conscription into the Egyptian army. Later there were rebellions and Transjordan became very dangerous for the traveller. By 1840 visitors to the Holy Land dared not cross the Jordan.

After the withdrawal of the Egyptian forces in 1840, some of them through Hesban, Ottoman rule returned to outlying areas only very slowly. "Another vast nomadic area which the Ottomans did not manage to subdue and control during the whole period [i.e., to 1861] was the area East of Jordan" (Ma'oz 1968: 145). Officials located in the northern town of Irbid served as some evidence of central authority, and several years later al-Kerak fell under Ottoman rule. However, the southern part of Jordan remained free of all government until 1894 (Ma'oz 1968: 145). The Ottomans failed to control the Bedouin as successfully as had the Egyptians, but not because of an inability to maintain military pressure on the tribesmen. Instead, the chief defect was the nature of the Ottoman administration itself. Ambivalent and unsystematic, Ottoman policy injudiciously utilized both conciliation and force. However, military measures were sporadic and incomplete, and flattery could not succeed without its steady military backing (Ma'oz 1968: 134).

In the 19th century, Hesban lay in an area slightly inhabited by two different tribes, the 'Ajarma (Ajarmeh), and the larger, stronger, 'Adwān (Adwan). The two tribes are discussed by Peake (n.d.: 168-174), and Jaussen (1908: 399-400). Only seminomadic, these tribes regularly cultivated the more productive bits of land, and found enough arable to redistribute it frequently within the tribe (Jaussen 1908: 238). Themselves composed of different groups lacking a common ancestor, the tribes lived in relative peace with each other. Generally the two tribes treated each other amicably, with the *shaykh*, or chief, of the Adwan ruling the area. By the end of the 19th century, the Adwan were considerably weaker than formerly, when they had terrorized areas as far away as Jerusalem. The tribe had also split into two groups, the larger under Shaykh 'Ali Diyāb (also spelled Dhiyab, etc.), who often camped at Hesban or its spring during the warmer months, and the Jordan Valley in winter.

A far fiercer tribe of nomads inhabited the area just east of Hesban. These were the Beni Sakhr, originally from the Hijaz. The date of their arrival on the Jordanian Plateau is disputed. Ma'oz (1968: 130) follows other historians and travellers who without much evidence claim that the tribe migrated from the Hijaz in the 18th century. Bakhit, on the other hand, shows that they held lands in Palestine long before that (1972: 226), and probably the Beni Sakhr frequented pasturages in Jordan in Mamluk times. Regardless of the date of their arrival, by the 19th century, the Beni Sakhr numbered perhaps five times as many tents as 'Ali Diyāb's Adwan, according to figures recorded by Jaussen. Very mobile and feared raiders in the true Bedouin tradition, they roamed the neighborhood, probably attracted in part by the spring of Hesban. So great a threat were the Beni Sakhr to the Adwan that when Ottoman officials in the late 19th century registered lands as Ajarmeh that had been Adwan for centuries, the Adwan did not contest the registration, for they needed Ajarmeh cooperation against the Beni Sakhr (Conder 1892: 322). Later 'Ali Diyāb complained of the injustice.

In turn, the Beni Sakhr faced rivals among the larger desert tribes. In 1880 there were invasions by Ibn Rashid, out of Central Arabia. As late as 1910 the Huwaytat under 'Awda abū Tāyyih avenged one loss by attacking the Beni Sakhr and driving them back to Hesban (Conder 1892: 317; Peake n.d.: 233).

Literary references to Hesban, unknown since Mamluk times, return with accounts by Western travellers in the 19th century[2]. They frequently remark on the number of tents at the site, or the ruins of the "castle" (Chesney 1868: 39). A more thorough survey of the area concluded that the ruins of Hesban, high above the spring, held no special interest (Conder 1892: 317). Early in the 20th century Elizabeth Bell, the noted English Orientalist, also stopped there, and pronounced the shaykh, Sultan, son of 'Ali Diyāb, "a proper rogue" (Bell 1907: 16).

Trade also expanded, and the Bedouin of the plateau could now mortgage their lands for food supplies in times of famine. In the case of Hesban, the Adwan and Ajarmeh Bedouin who owned the farmland fell into debt to Nabulsi, a merchant in al-Salt. Eventually, they proved unable to finance their mortgages, and Nabulsi bought their lands. He personally did not cultivate the fields around Hesban; this was the work of Bedouins, then later migrant workers from the Ghor (Jordan Valley) and West Bank.

The imposition of Ottoman rule was not always peaceful. Along with stability and an end to raiding, Ottoman rule brought taxes and conscription. The latter appears to have been a motivating factor behind revolts in al-Shawbak (1905) and al-Kerak (1910) (Al-Mādī and Mūsā 1959: 18-26; Kazziha 1972).

The years just before World War I witnessed an increasing Ottoman control over Transjordan. Along the edge of the desert, the pilgrim railway to Medina was constructed, running through Mafraq, Amman, and Ma'an. Better transportation and general modernization furnished to control the area, and enabled it to crush resistance. As a result, municipal government began, and by 1913 Madaba gained both a mayor and a city council ('Uzayzi 1978 interview). Hesban, however, remained largely a tent-site.

After the Ottoman Empire entered World War I on the side of the Central Powers, the inhabitants of the Belqa began a period of considerable suffering and deprivation. The unexpected vitality of the Turkish armies in the first years of the war, as well as the unsuccessful attempts to capture the Suez Canal, imposed considerable burdens upon the inhabitants of Syria in general. In border areas like Palestine and Transjordan, military needs were particularly great, as the recollections of the author Ruks al-Uzayzi indicate. Born and raised in Madaba, al-Uzayzi remembers that beginning one morning, the Turkish authorities began requisitioning things from the village. First labor, then donkeys, and later camels were also taken. While the men were largely absent, the houses were searched several times for flax and wheat. These were seized, and available horses "purchased" with the rapidly-depreciating Ottoman paper money. Later that same afternoon, more men were requisitioned to fight the locust hordes then invading Syria ('Uzayzi 1978 interview). This account, plus widespread conscription, indicate the major causes of suffering. Because food grains could not be imported, and the locusts devoured local crops in 1916 and 1917, malnutrition and poverty were extensive. However, the Belqa escaped the starvation that decimated the population of Lebanon and elsewhere and witnessed little fighting.

For almost the entire course of the war, Hesban lay behind the Ottoman lines, with Hijazi (Arab) regulars fighting to the south, a mobile Arab strike force to the east, and the British forces in Palestine to the west. Perhaps T. E. Lawrence passed by the spot while on a journey behind enemy lines. He did visit Madaba, and although he fails to mention Hesban in *Seven Pillars of Wisdom*, Robert Graves' book *Lawrence and the Arabian Adventure* has maps showing the eccentric Englishman passing by.

With the decisive British breakthrough in Palestine in September 1918, and the subsequent arrival of British troops at Madaba, Ottoman rule over Hesban ended, and Arab rule began.

The Modern Arab Period: 1918-Present

Even before the war ended, the Allied commander General Edmund Allenby divided the captured areas of geographical Syria into administrative districts. For political as well as military reasons, the Arab forces received the interior, from southern Jordan north to the Turkish-speaking areas beyond Aleppo, to govern until the Peace Conference settled the status of the area. This Arab administration, with its capital at Damascus and led by Faysal ibn al-Husayn, became the direct foundation for the present state of Jordan.

At first, the Arab government faced immense problems with few resources and vast handicaps. The first civil and military governor, Ja'far al-'Askari, fell ill and proved ineffective. His control was also weakened by the rugged nature of the countryside and an absolute dearth of funds. In early 1919, the Arab government in Damascus found itself destitute, and unable even to provide a modest sum to feed the starving around the town of al-Salt whose crops had been damaged by fighting in the spring and fall of 1918. Naturally it took time for the first modern Arab state to establish itself and extend its authority. Meanwhile, in Transjordan the settled inhabitants suffered incursions by the Beni Sakhr and other Bedouins, wartime allies of the Arab Revolt who now obstructed the desires of the Arab state to establish law and order. Not surprisingly, the inhabitants remained armed throughout the period of Arab rule. This era ended in July, 1920, when the French invading force defeated the Arab army outside Damascus, and the Arab kingdom quickly disintegrated (Al-Mādī and Mūsā 1959; Russell 1977).

Ejected from the Syrian capital, Faysal left the Middle East for Europe, and the government of Transjordan fell into a limbo of sorts. The French forces did not occupy areas south of the present Syrian-Jordanian border, and the East Bank lapsed into zones of local government. Many of the officials had served the Arab government in Transjordan or elsewhere, and they now attempted to maintain order, often with British liaison officers operating behind the scenes. Hesban and the rest of the Belqa fell under the control of Mazhar Raslān, whose capital was al-Salt (Al-Mādī and Mūsā 1959: 115).

International events, however, soon caused a change in these arrangements. The San Remo Conference of Allied leaders gave Britain the mandate for Palestine and Transjordan. However, because of a number of previous promises, announcements, and agreements, Britain did not attempt to impose direct rule over Transjordan. Instead, British officials desired a form of indirect rule over an Arab government there, and they soon found an obvious candidate of nationalist and Hashemite credentials to govern the area. Amir Abdullah, the second son of King Husayn of the Hijaz and older brother of Faysal, appeared in southern Transjordan in 1921, initially to drive the French out of Syria. However, he eventually proved willing to sacrifice the somewhat hopeless cause of his brother's throne for an opportunity to govern the often unruly population of Transjordan. With British approval and involvement, the Amirate of Trans-Jordan was established in 1921, and Abdullah's Hashemite family has continued to rule to the present, gaining full independence in 1946.

Despite its longevity, Hashemite rule initially proved difficult to establish. There were Bedouin attacks by Wahhabis from the Hijaz, and a number of disturbances broke out in remote areas. Perhaps the boldest challenge, however, originated at Hesban not far from Abdullah's capital of Amman. Early in September, 1923, a number of men opposed to Abdullah met at Hesban, summoned by Sultan, shaykh of the Adwan.

Learning that they were to be arrested for scheming rebellion, the plotters and fighting men of the Adwan tribe left Hesban on September 6, calling other tribes to battle for the freedom enjoyed under the previous system of local governments. Initial successes brought the rebels to the vicinity of Amman, but after the unexpected arrival of a British armored car and the subsequent killing of one of the leaders of the revolt, Sāyil al-Shahwāh, shaykh of the Ajarmeh, the rebellion quickly collapsed (Al-Mādī and Mūsā 1959: 217-218). Some suggest that the role of the armored car was unexpected by the rebels because the British instigated them, favoring the form of local rule that could be controlled more easily than the nationalist Abdullah.

Only after the firm establishment of Abdullah's rule did Hesban slowly begin to grow as a permanent village. By then the Nabulsi family had lived there for a generation, often employing imported or migrant labor to till the fields originally belonging to the Adwan and Ajarmeh Bedouin. Gradually the population of the area increased, forcing a change in the methods of production and forcing more and more nomads to abandon grazing and their herds in favor of permanent cultivation. The figures are sketchy, but Conder (1892: 321) estimated the whole Belqa population in the 1880s at something around 11,000. In contrast, the present population of the Amman area alone substantially exceeds one million, swollen both by natural increase on the East Bank and refugees from Palestine. Nevertheless, until very recently—the 1960s perhaps—Hesban remained a small village, dominated by the houses of the Nabulsi landowners. The first school began only in 1948, and a paved road reached Hesban only in the late 1960s. Travel was therefore limited, and the tenant farmers who lived there faced few opportunities for education and advancement. The remainder of this chapter will consider the present town, based largely on interviews with members of the Nabulsi family and several inhabitants, including Mahmūd and Muhammad al-Barārī and 'Abd al-Rahmān Masha'lī.

Hesban Today[3]

Today a variety of crops are cultivated in the lands surrounding Hesban. In place of the great dependence on wheat and barley grown as subsistence crops earlier this century, a number of cash crops are produced, including tomatoes, lentils, melons, and some grains. The average annual rainfall amounts to around 350-400 mm, enough in good years to produce ample crops without irrigation. The high clay content of the soil retains considerable moisture, and thus some harvest may result even in drier years. Besides following a rotation system that leaves one-third of the land fallow, farmers use some fertilizers, but little irrigation, as the water-pipe running past the village generally is empty.

As in the past three-quarters of a century, the Nabulsi family owns most of the surrounding lands. The present owners are the grandsons, generally, of the original merchant, and what were once large fields have often been subdivided into as many as six sections. Needless to say, the traditional practice ("musha'") of periodically redistributing lands among members of the tribe who cultivate them has been abandoned completely. Ownership remains in the hands of the Nabulsis, most of them absentee landlords following their various professions in Amman.

The Nabulsis nevertheless retain a strong interest in their lands, and the sharecroppers who farm them are often old acquaintances. Like most of the 2,000 or so inhabitants of Hesban, these farmers descended mostly from the Ajarmeh tribe, plus some Adwan and others. In return for raising a crop, the sharecropper will split the proceeds evenly with the Nabulsi owner, although the terms will vary, depending on the land's fertility and whether machinery can be used. (The landlord, of course, receives nothing on the third of his land that must lie fallow each year.)

Within the village, the houses are generally built of cement block, on land owned by the householder. The adjoining gardens, with a few vines and olive trees, represent a fairly recent phenomenon: thirty years ago there were no fruit trees. Several villagers feel that these innovations, like the cash crops, are because of greater knowledge and innovation on the part of the farmers and not a result of any government agricultural programs.

Although lying in an agricultural area, the village of Hesban is more than a farming community. Today many of the inhabitants work in Amman, and in fact at certain seasons like the lentil harvest there is a distinct shortage of manpower. Regardless of profession, large families are the rule in this completely Muslim village. Eight to twelve children are average, and polygamy is practiced by men who have both the inclination and the means. Children of both sexes now receive their primary education within the village, but the secondary school is for boys only. At considerable expense and hardship to themselves, some families educate their daughters at the girls' secondary school in Madaba. In a culture where the previous generation of women expected no employment outside the home, this is proof of a remarkable change in thinking, unaccompanied by much propaganda, government or otherwise. Another sign of the strong current of modernization is the great desire of families to send their sons to the University of Jordan, despite the great expenses involved. It is commonly recognized, according to Hasan Nabulsi, recent Secretary-General of the University, that families will even sacrifice family food to provide a higher education for their children. In time this trend of greater education may, both directly and indirectly, through changes in values, affect family size. Already the average marriage age has climbed to 24 or 25 for males, after education, accumulation of some savings, and possibly military service.

Aside from the schools and post office, there is little evidence of the central government in the village of

Hesban. There are telephones, but electricity has not yet arrived, and such television sets as obviously exist are powered either by batteries or privately-owned generators. Although in the broad sense the government supplies protection, there are no local police. At least some of the Nabulsi family and a number of farmers consider the local town council, or *majlis*, relatively ineffective. There is no hospital; indeed, several residents hoped that in return for the archaeological sites supplied by the village, the American excavators might furnish a clinic, not through the government, but directly to the people.

In many ways, modern Hesban shares its social, economic, and cultural features with other small villages and towns around Amman. Like them its residents generally take little part in politics, due in part to the present circumstances in Jordan. However, Hesban is unique in one way. Having served as a basis for the plotters of 1923, it also supplied Jordan with the nationalist and moderately socialist politician Sulaymān al-Nabulsi. In 1956, he was elected Prime Minister of the kingdom, but his activities and beliefs threatened the monarchy itself, and King Husayn removed Nabulsi from office in 1957.

Conclusion

The salient features of Islamic rule over Jordan must be stressed. Following the Arab conquest, the lower classes remained on the land, and gradually exchanged their Aramaic for Arabic, their Christianity for Islam. In government, the initial form of mixed Arab and Byzantine forms gradually yielded under the Abbasids to a strictly Muslim rule, then to domination by various local rulers. In part because of these changes, in part possibly because of changes in world trade routes or the average annual precipitation, the population of the East Bank declined. This decline changed the nature of food production, and in turn the inhabitants abandoned houses for tents. This further reduced government control, and by the middle Ottoman Period Hesban and the surrounding areas were governed only by the unwritten laws of the desert. This period was not one of total isolation from the outside world. New products such as tobacco and the tomato came into use. Coffee, though originally from the Middle East, became far more important following its cheaper production in South America.

Economic and social change accelerated greatly in the 19th and 20th centuries, following the establishment of law and order and a return of permanent settlement. Again the changes in governmental control and population density forced a shift in methods of food production. As a result, the population of the region quickly surpassed its Byzantine height. Hesban reflects all this with its transformation from a place of tents to a village boasting televisions and cars; with left-wing politics replacing the countless Bedouin conflicts of the past. However, over the present inhabitants must hang three

important limitations on the future. First, a climate that yields so little rain will limit the size of population in both village and region. Second, a strong governmental authority, so vital to sedentary farmers in the past, must continue or herding may again replace cultivation. Finally, a solution of the Palestine problem that resulted in market competition from farmers in the better-watered lands west of the Jordan might plunge the whole East Bank into agricultural difficulties.

References[4]

Abū al-Fidā'
    1840 *Kitāb Taqwīm al-Buldān*. Paris: Royal Press, reprinted Baghdad: Maktaba al-Mithna, 1963.

Ashtor, E.
    1976 *A Social and Economic History of the Near East in the Middle Ages*. London: Collins.

Al-Bakhīt, M. A.
    1976 *Mamlakat al-Karak*. Amman: n.p.

[Bakhit, M. A.]
    1972 *The Ottoman Province of Damascus in the Sixteenth Century*. Ph.D. Thesis. London: School of Oriental and Asian Studies.

Barkan, O. L.
    1958 "Essai sur les données statistiques des registres de recensement dans l'empire ottoman aux XVe et XVIe siècles." *Journal of the Economic and Social History of the Orient*. I: 9-36.

Behâ ed-Dîn [Bahā' al-Dīn]
    1897 *The Life of Saladin*. Trans. C. R. Conder from French. Vol. 13 of the library of the Palestine Pilgrims' Text Society. London: Palestine Pilgrims' Text Society.

Bell, G. L.
    1907 *Syria: The Desert and the Sown*. New York: Dutton.

Brice, W. C.
    1978 *The Environmental History of the Near and Middle East Since the Last Ice Age*. London: Academic Press.

Chesney, F. R.
    1868 *Narrative of the Euphrates Expedition*. London: Longmans, Green.

Conder, C. R.
    1892 *Heth and Moab: Explorations in Syria in 1881 and 1882*. London: Macmillan.

Dols, M. W.
    1977 *The Black Death in the Middle East*. Princeton: Princeton University.

Harding, G. L.
1960 "'Amman," *Encyclopaedia of Islam*, New Edition [EI₂]. Leiden: Brill.

Heidet, L.
1903 Hésébon. Cols. 657-663 in vol. 3 of *Dictionnaire de la Bible*, ed. F. G. Vigouroux. Paris: Letouzey et Ané.

Hitti, P. K.
1957 *History of Syria Including Lebanon and Palestine*. London: Macmillan.

Ibn Jubayr
1964 *Rihlat Ibn Jubayr*. Beirut: Dar Sadir.

Ibn Sasrā
1963 *Al-Durra al-Mudi'a fi al-Dawla al-Zahiriya*. Trans. William Brinner from Arabic. Berkeley: University of California.

Ibn Tūlūn
1952 *Les Gouverneurs de Damas sous les Mamlouks et les premiers Ottomans*. Trans. Henri Laoust from Arabic. Damascus: Institut français de Damas.

Jaussen, A.
1908 *Coutumes des Arabes au pays de Moab*. Paris: Librairie Lecoffre.

Kahāla, U. R.
n.d. *Mu'jam al-Mu'allifin*. Beirut: Maktabat al-Mathani.

Kazziha, W.
1972 *The Social History of Southern Syria (Trans-Jordan) in the 19th and Early 20th Century*. Beirut: Arab University.

Le Strange, G.
1965 *Palestine Under the Moslems: A Description of Syria and the Holy Land from A.D. 650 to 1500*. Beirut: Khayats.

Al-Mādī, M., and Mūsā, S.
1959 *Tarikh al-Urdann fi al-Qarn al-'Ishrin*. Amman: n.p.

Ma'oz, M.
1968 *Ottoman Reform in Syria and Palestine, 1840-1861*. Oxford: Clarendon.

Mansi, J. D., ed.
1960 *Sacrorum Conciliorum Nova et Amplissima Collectio*, vol. 10. Graz (Austria): Akademische Druck-Verlagsanstalt.

Al-Maqrīzī
1837 *Histoire des sultans mamlouks d'Egypte*. Trans. Etienne Quatremère from Arabic. Paris: Oriental Translation Fund.

Muir, W.
1968 *The Mameluke or Slave Dynasty of Egypt, AD 1260-1517*. Amsterdam: Oriental.

Peake, F.
n.d. *Tarikh Sharqi al-Urdann wa Qabā'iliha*. Ed. and Trans. Bahā' al-Dīn Tuqan from English.

1958 *A History of Jordan and Its Tribes*. Coral Gables, FL: University of Miami.

Rafeq, Abdul-Karim
1970 *The Province of Damascus: 1723-1783*. Beirut: Khayats.

Russell, M. B.
1977 Towards an Arab State: The Syrian Administration, 1918-1920. Unpublished paper, Andrews University, Berrien Springs, MI.

Saba, G., and 'Uzayzi, R.
1961 *Ma'dabā wa Dūwāḥiha*. Jerusalem: Matba' al-Ābā' al-Yusu 'īyīn.

Sourdel-Thomine, J.
1960 "Al-Balkā'." *Encyclopaedia of Islam*, New Edition [EI₂]. Leiden: Brill.

Stevenson, W. L.
1907 *The Crusaders in the East*. Cambridge: University. Reprinted Librairie du Liban.

Al-Tabari [At-Ṭabarī]
1964 *Annales quos scripsit Abu Djafar Mohammed ibn Djarir at-Tabari*. Ed. and Trans. M. J. De Goeje from Arabic. Leiden: Brill.

Yāqūt
1866 *Kitab Mu'jam al-Buldan*. Ed. Ferdinand Wustenfeld. Leipzig; reprinted Tehran, 1965.

Ziadeh, N. A.
1953 *Urban Life in Syria Under the Early Mamlūks*. Beirut: American.

Endnotes

[1]Husbān is the classical Arab pronunciation of the name, now modified to "Hisban." "Hesban," the spelling adopted by the archaeologists, has been retained here for continuity, as has Belqa for Balqā', and other Anglicized names given in parentheses.

[2]For a detailed account of the reports of visitors to Hesban in the 19th and 20th centuries, see Appendix B in this book.

[3]This was written in 1978 and so does not take into consideration the changes that have occurred at Hesban since then.

[4]The names of Arabic authors that begin with the article al (or at) are alphabetized according to the initial of the name proper.

Chapter Three

A REVIEW OF CRITICAL STUDIES OF
OLD TESTAMENT REFERENCES TO HESHBON

Arthur J. Ferch

Chapter Three

A Review of Critical Studies of
Old Testament References to Heshbon

Introduction

There are thirty-eight references to Heshbon in the OT (Num 21:25, 26, 27, 28, 30, 34; 32:3, 37; Deut 1:4; 2:24, 26, 30; 3:2, 6; 4:46; 29:7 [H 29:6]; Josh 9:10; 12:2, 5; 13:10, 17, 21, 26, 27; 21:39; Judg 11:19, 26; Isa 15:4; 16:8, 9; Jer 48:2, 34, 45 (2x); 49:3; Cant 7:4 [H 7:5]; Neh 9:22; 1 Chr 6:81 [H 6:66]. Most of these passages report or allude to the Israelite defeat of Sihon, an Amorite king of Heshbon during the conquest period and the subsequent settlement of the lower half of the Transjordan by the tribes Reuben and Gad. The references to Heshbon in Isaiah and Jeremiah occur in elegies upon the fate of Moab (except Jer 49:3, which is part of an oracle on Ammon) which unfortunately provide insufficient data for purposes of precise dating. Since critical studies during the past century dealing with OT references to Heshbon have shown interest primarily in the Sihon conquest traditions (recorded in Num 21, Deut 2, and Judg 11) and specifically the poem of Heshbon (Num 21:27-30), the present study will limit itself mainly to a critical evaluation of scholarly treatments of these accounts.

A Review of Critical Studies

The customary interpretation of the song of Heshbon prior to 1881 (Baentsch 1903: 585) is reflected in the view advanced by H. Ewald (1883: 205-207). Ewald suggested that Num 21:27-30 "springs directly from the very first period of the conquest" and represents an Israelite song of victory which taunts the subdued Amorites (205-207). Ewald retained the phrase "to an Amorite king, Sihon" in vs. 29d and understood vs. 30 as a personal reference to Israel. Accordingly, he interpreted vs. 27 as an Israelite scornful summons in which the defeated Amorites are challenged to rebuild their ruined capital Heshbon—if they can. A second voice then utters the woe-saying on Moab in vss. 28-29 commemorating the Amorite victory over Moab, in order to magnify the present Israelite conquest. The focus reverts back to the Israelites, who in vs. 30 rejoice over their own victory over the Amorites (205-206). This song then was the expression of feelings which crowded in upon the youthful and victorious Israelites after their victory over Sihon at Jahaz reported in the accompanying prose narrative of Num 21:21-31 (205).

In 1881 Meyer (117-146), in a critique of biblical reports dealing with the conquest of Palestine, briefly discussed the song of Heshbon and for the first time (Baentsch 1903: 582) challenged the prevailing interpretation of the poem as represented by Ewald. He claimed that Sihon was a Moabite king and proposed that the song described the rather drawn-out battles fought between Israel and Moab during the time of Omri (131). Meyer's suggestion, championed by Stade (1881: 146), asserted that Num 21:27-30 had nothing to do with the Amorites for the following reasons:

1. Jer 48:45-47, which in part represents the same reading as Num 21:27-30, is definitely addressed to Moabites, hence the poem in Numbers speaks to the same people;

2. the clause "to an Amorite king, Sihon" of vs. 29d disturbs the parallelism (by which Meyer seems to mean the meter) of the poem and contradicts the rest of this song (on his supposition that these verses referred to the Moabites); and

3. the colon "[from] Heshbon to Dibon" designates a north-to-south movement which contradicts the south-to-north direction of the surrounding narrative but comports with an Omride Israelite conquest moving southward (131).

As for the "unhistorical" narrative Num 21:21-26, vs. 24b is a gloss looking forward to vs. 32 (120), and vs. 26 an interpolation to justify Israel's possession of land which belonged to Moab (129-131).

Meyer presumed that the song of Heshbon was derived from a 9th-century collection of national martial hymns (viz., the "Book of the Wars of Yahweh") and misunderstood by the 8th-century B.C. Elohist source which erroneously applied the account to the time of Moses (131-132). In 1885 Meyer published a defense of his proposal (36-52) against the dissenting opinion of A. Kuenen; however, no new significant arguments were added to his 1881 statement.

Meyer's opinion was essentially supported by B. Baentsch in 1903 (581-587). Baentsch observed that though Meyer and Stade had given the impression that the Amorite kingdom was a purely imaginary dominion, the existence of Amorites could be traced at least to the 15th century B.C. (582, *cf.* Holzinger 1903: 99).

Authors now had to come to terms with the interpretations of the Sihon tradition represented by Ewald and Meyer. Both A. Dillmann (1886: 128-133) and G. A. Smith (n.d.: 560, 662-664) substantially agreed with Ewald. Dillmann dismissed Meyer's explanation of both vss. 24b and 26 (128-129) and the poem by observing that such a claim for the song "imputirt ohne allen Grund nicht bloss dem Schriftsteller ein sehr leichtsinniges Verfahren, sondern auch den ursprünglichen Lesern seines Buchs eine unglaubliche Gedankenlosigkeit, welcher sich alles bieten liess" (133). Smith contended for the integrity of the Sihon account and insisted that the song of Heshbon was a taunt of the victorious Israelites challenging the Amorites to return and rebuild Heshbon.

Against Meyer, Smith argued that the date of the document, which contains the poem,

at the latest in eighth century, forbids that its authors could have confused a war in the ninth century with one in the fourteenth. . . . Moreover, such an invasion of Eastern Palestine by the Amorites of the west was possible; while it is impossible to understand, if the facts were not as stated, any motive for the invention of the tale (561).

The Sihon clause in vs. 29d should be retained since "there is no objection, apart from the requirements of this theory" (664). He added:

To sum up: the theory of Meyer and Stade, that the war with Sihon is unhistorical, and that the poem refers to a conquest by Israel of Moab in the ninth century, can only be held by sacrificing vv. 26 and 29d, against neither of which is there any objection apart from this theory . . . (664).

While a number of Smith's and Dillmann's objections have to be taken seriously, it is regrettable that neither addressed himself to the question of meter in vs. 29d.

In 1903 three commentaries on Numbers came off the presses, two in German (Baentsch and Holzinger) and one in English (Gray). Baentsch, as noted above, aligned himself largely with Meyer and Stade. While Baentsch agreed with Ewald and Meyer that vs. 30 represented the Israelites speaking of themselves, he decided with Meyer that the poem was a depiction of Israelite engagements with the Moabites during the Omride period (586-587). He explained, ignoring objections which had by now been raised, that Israelites no longer remembered the details of their early wars and fused their rather vague memory of these with the combats of Omri in such a way that the former outline was painted with the colors of the latter. Baentsch was certain that the Heshbon account had nothing to do with the Amorites. This evaluation had serious repercussions for the accompanying narrative since the poem was taken to be the source for the surrounding narrative.

While Holzinger's comments on Num 21:21-31 (1903: 98-100) are somewhat indecisive and imprecise, he seems inclined to think that the poem originally referred to an Amorite victory but was reinterpreted as an Israelite taunt as it entered the Elohist source (cf. Hanson 1968: 293). Gray (1903: 300-307), on the other hand, examined the views of both Ewald and Meyer and decided that because of ambiguities in interpretation "the one thing that is clear is that the poem celebrates a victory over Moab" (1903: 300). He considered Ewald's view improbable because it required a strong antithesis in vs. 30. Gray concluded that though the text of vs. 30 is corrupt,

one thing is certain: it does not contain an emphatic antithesis. . . . There is not the slightest indication that the conquerors of v. 30 are different from those who are represented as conquerors in v. 27f., and consequently the poem itself contains no indication that v. 27f. are tauntingly spoken (301).

As for Meyer's theory, Gray recognized that:

it is not without difficulties, though the necessity for regarding v. 29e as a gloss is scarcely one of these. The chief difficulty lies in the fact that the natural, though perhaps not the inevitable, inference is that Sihon was actually a king of *Moab*, and only became turned into a king of the Amorites in later traditions (301).

With the interest in geography, topography, and archaeology of the Transjordan region and further research into OT criticism in the late thirties and early forties of the present century, the Heshbon accounts again received notice (*e.g.* Abel 1933, 1938; Heinisch 1936: 84; Rudolph 1938: 39-40; Glueck, esp. 1940: 137-140; de Vaux 1941: 16-25; Noth 1940: 161-189, 1944: 11-57, 1968: 160-67).[1] Glueck, while not entering into the literary critical debate, accepted the essential integrity of the Heshbon accounts and placed the story in the 13th-century B.C. conquest setting. De Vaux and Noth equally accepted the substantial antiquity of the materials (de Vaux 1978: 564-567; Noth 1972: 73).

De Vaux suggested that "both Deut 2:26-26 [sic.] and Judges 11:19-21 are derived from Num 21:21-31, the first simply adding a theological interpretation to the story and the second summarizing the longer earlier account" (564). The historical meaning of Num 21:21-31, de Vaux argued, "depends to a very great extent on how the poem contained in verses 27b-30 is interpreted. Unfortunately, the crucial verse 30 is corrupt" (565). De Vaux rejected the ideas that the poem was originally an Amorite victory song and that it was a song "celebrating the defeat of the Moabites by a king of Israel, either Omri or David" (565). Like Gray, he contends that the latter view does nothing to explain the references in the poem to Sihon. Instead, he aligns himself with Ewald (also Rudolph and Noth), insisting that the poem celebrates the Israelite success in the period of the conquest (565).

De Vaux further argues that at the time of Israel's victory, Sihon's "kingdom did not extend very far to the north of Heshbon" (566; *cf.* de Vaux 1941: 16-25). Though he concedes that Sihon may have exercised a measure of control over the nomads north of his kingdom, he concludes that the references to Sihon's territory extending from the Arnon to the Jabbok (in Num 21:26 and Josh 12:2-3) "have probably been a-dapted to provide an idealized frontier" (566).[2]

A more striking reconstruction of the Sihon tradition was proposed by Noth. While in essence agreeing with Ewald, he introduced a number of substantial modifications. Noth's discussion of the Heshbon narratives occurs in the broader context of his traditio-historical analyses and investigations into the settlement process of the Transjordan region.

In his research into the Sihon tradition Noth focused particularly on Num 21:21-31, and though admitting to some unevenness in vss. 24-25 (arguments which can be traced back to Meyer [1881: 120] and Baentsch [1903: 581-583]), contended strongly for the basic unity of this pericope (1940: 164).[3] With the majority of scholars before him, Noth agreed that Num 21 originated from the ancient Elohist source.[4] The reason for this judgment was the general designation of the pre-Israelite inhabitants of the land as Amorites (163-164, 182-192). In this judgment he had been anticipated by Meyer (1881: 121-122).[5]

Noth observed that as the author inserted the older poetic song (Num 21:27-30) into the later surrounding narrative he added vss. 25-26 as explanatory and transitory remarks. Though these transitory verses repeated some earlier elements he argued that this in no way characterized them as doublets and grounds for source division (1940: 166).

The song of Heshbon is an Israelite victory song which incorporates a dirge in vss. 28-29. Verses 27 and 30 represent Reuben-Gad's conquest of Sihon while vss. 28-29 depict Sihon's success over Moab prior to the Israelite assault. Hence the verbs in vss. 28-29 should be rendered pluperfect in tense. Though with Meyer, Noth omitted the words "king Sihon" from vs. 29d (retaining "Amorite"), he rejected the monarchical or later settings for the song because no cogent reasons had been advanced for the latter (1944: 39). The puzzling *wannîrām* and *wannaššîm* in vs. 30 Noth translated as *imperfecta consecutiva* describing the Israelites in contrast to the Amorites in vs. 29. His emended vs. 30 then reads:

> But we have gained the upper hand, Heshbon is ruined and we have further kindled a fire against Medeba (1968: 161).

This song, then, an element of genuine Israelite tradition (1940: 169) and not misunderstood as completely as is often assumed, can serve as the oldest source for the settlement in the Transjordan. Indeed Noth took this poem as a clue for his rearrangement of the canonical context and historical reconstruction of events related to the biblical conquest. While Noth acknowledged that the biblical order of events, which records first the victory over Sihon (Num 21:21-31), then the conquest of Jazer (vs. 32), and finally, the settlement of Reuben-Gad, is not impossible (1944:

39), he suggested that this order was brought about by the later conception of a united Israel moving from the south to the north.

He observed the north-to-south movement of the poem and sought to detect and arrange passages which would suit a southward thrust of Israelites in the Transjordan. Having inferred a rather complex history of settlement, Noth dismissed both the accounts in Josh 13:15-23, 24-28 and the reports of settlement in this area reflected in Deuteronomy-Kings because the former reflects tribal geographical theories while the latter is a simplification and schematization of the historical narrative (1944: 13-17, 52).

From references to the "plain of Moab," the "land of Moab," and the Balaam account (Num 22-24), Noth deduces that the Moabites had originally lived not only north of the Arnon but also along the eastern shore of the Dead Sea as comparatively permanent neighbors of Reuben-Gad (1944: 18-38). After excising the phrase "in the land of Gilead" as either erroneous or a later gloss (36), Noth uses Num 32:1 as evidence that Reuben-Gad initially settled in Jazer. He rejects the information in Num 22:1 that the Israelites lived in the "plains of Moab" and instead submits a locality north or northeast of Peor which would be met by his identification of Jazer (26-28, 31-36).

In time, Noth postulates, Reuben-Gad expanded their territory southward and thus came in contact with Sihon of Heshbon. Though Noth sees no reason to doubt the originality of the phrase "from the Arnon to the Jabbok" (1944: 38, 1940: 164-165) he prefers to view it as a redactional gloss taken over from Deut 3:16.[6] Thus, against Glueck, Noth and de Vaux considerably narrow the boundaries of the Sihon state. It is this southern expansion by Reuben-Gad which Noth sees reflected in the song of Heshbon, the narrative enclosing the song, and Moses' speech in Deut 2:26-37 (1944: 37). Omitting the reference to Dibon in Num 21:30 as another later addition (39 n. 1; 1968: 161), Noth advocates a subsequent extension by Reuben-Gad as far as Madaba. Indeed, he thinks, the land right down to the Arnon may not have been Israel's until after David's victory over Moab (2 Sam 8:2; 1944: 42).

Noth's rather unique reconstruction depends on the validity and cogency of his textual emendations, proposed redactional glosses, his interpretation of the poem and complete reversal of the canonical historical order. Though a number of critics questioned Noth's attribution of Num 21:21-31 to the Elohist source (*e.g.* de Vaux 1978: 565; Van Seters 1972: 182), and recent advances in OT criticism have called into question the canons of accepted Pentateuchal criticism,[7] there at least appears nothing that significantly contests his claim that the passage essentially is a literary unity and represents a genuine ancient Israelite tradition. Noth also appears to be right in his estimate that there are no cogent reasons for a monarchical setting for Num 21. Similarly, the references to the "land of Moab," "the plain of Moab," and Balak's rather easy access to the area north of the Arnon cannot be ignored. However, his conclusion that this proves a settled Moabite population in this area assumes too much. A better explanation may be Smith's (Smith n.d.: 663) interpretation that

> though Moab had been driven out by Sihon from her proper territory, her name would more or less remain attached to it; so that though the place Israel encamped on opposite Jericho was called Arboth-Moab, that need not mean that Moab still possessed it. Dillmann, too, points out that Sihon's conquest of Heshbon need not be taken to mean that all the Moabites were banished.

Though Noth's preferred interpretation of the phrase "from the Arnon to the Jabbok" does not appear too compelling, his arguments have at least shown that the borders must be understood far more flexibly. Indeed, Sihon's kingdom may have resembled more a tribal holding with relatively unstable borders resembling "Israel" prior to the term's becoming a rather precise geographical denotation during the monarchy (Bright 1972: 197).

It is difficult, nevertheless, to escape the suspicion that a number of Noth's proposed emendations were elicited less by decisive textual, literary-critical or traditio-historical problems than by his proposed historical order of events (*cf. e.g.*, his argument for Jahaz as a later gloss in Num 21:23; his reasons for omitting Dibon and the considerable conjectures associated with Num 21:30; the rather forced explanation of Num 22:1 and the grounds for omitting "Gilead" in Num 32:1). De Vaux, who is also committed to a premonarchial setting for the Heshbon tradition, remained unconvinced by Noth's theory that the tribes settled first in the Jazer district and gradually expanded southward. De Vaux contends that this hypothesis is

> contradicted by the only precise datum provided in Num 21:21-31 concerning the geography of the war waged against Sihon, namely that he was beaten at Jahaz (verse 23), the site of which is uncertain. According to this text in relation to Heshbon, Jahaz is in the direction of the desert, although not necessarily in the desert itself. At the time when Eusebius was writing (Onom 104, 11), Jahaz was believed to have been between Medeba and Dibon and, according to the Moabite Stone (1. 19-20), Mesha took it back and attached it to Dibon. This points to a site to the south-east of Heshbon, so that the Israelites must have attacked from the south and the attacking group must have come from the desert. We have no reason to doubt that this was the group led by Moses and that these Israelites reached the plain to the north-east of the Dead Sea by this route and crossed the Jordan from that point (1978: 566-567).

Though Noth dismissed this objection he gave no support for doing so.

Bartlett, a critic sympathetic to Noth, noted correctly that much of Noth's hypothesis depends upon his reconstruction and interpretation of the notorious *crux interpretum* vs. 30 (1969: 96-97). Bartlett contends that the application of vs. 30 to the Israelites is dubious and the consequent antithesis in the poem required by Noth's interpretation is missing. Actually there is no reason why Num 21:27-30 and vss. 21-25 need cover the same ground. These problems in Noth's understanding of the poem are not without repercussions on his historical reconstruction. Indeed the southward movement of the poem is equally applicable if the poem depicted the Amorite conquest of Moab before the putative Israelite subjugation of the Amorites. The cumulative force of questions and objections raised against Noth's emendations, glosses, and reordering of the narrative seem to be too serious to remain ignored.

In 1960 A. H. Van Zyl published a monograph about the Moabites. In this study Van Zyl utilized Num 21:21-31 alongside other sources to reconstruct a history of the Moabites (esp. 108-122). While providing neither a detailed exegesis nor a source-critical analysis of Num 21:21-31, Van Zyl noted that this Amorite defeat by the Israelites was given repeated attention in subsequent history (*cf*. Deut 2:24-36; 3:6, 8, 12; Josh 12:1-3; Judg 11:19-22).

He rejected the hypothesis that the song within the larger narrative of Num 21:21-31 was an Israelite satire taunting the Amorites with bitter scorn and only casually alluded to the Amorite triumph over the Moabites in order to boost Israelite achievements. Van Zyl remarked that the area in which the battle described in the song took place is not the same as that of the clash recounted in the prose narrative. Hence his conclusion that two different clashes must be spoken of in the poetic and prose accounts (8-10).

Van Zyl repudiated Meyer's theory because it required unwarranted alterations to the text. He agreed with Meyer as to the southward thrust of the troops in the poem but explained that this comported better with an Amorite conquest of Moab. Van Zyl's major objection to Meyer was that the transfer of the Sihon story to the period of Mesha conflicted with the historical context of the song, especially when there was no reason to doubt the historicity of the context (8-10). Unfortunately, Van Zyl did not respond to Meyer's charge that the Sihon clause in Num 21:29d overburdened the meter, but suggested that the song was originally intended to be an Amorite mocking song chanted by Amorite *mošelîm* after defeating the Moabites (9-10):

> This is indicated by the sarcastic invitation to Moab to return to the recently destroyed city of Heshbon and rebuild it. In ancient times the mocking song played a prominent part in warfare. This interpretation of the song conforms to its context, and it does not require inherent alterations of the text. By re-using this Amorite mocking song directed against the Moabites, the

Israelites by implication uttered a threat against Moab. Thus they urged the king of Moab to acquire the help of Balaam (10).

In his historical reconstruction Van Zyl submits that Moabite tribes lived not only south of the Arnon but also extended north of the river into territory controlled by the Amorites. Among the cities governed by the Moabites were Heshbon, Dibon, Madaba, and possibly Nophah. In the northwest Moabite influence reached to the "plain of Moab," a name which originated before Israel and Moab met in dispute.

The clash with the Amorites occurred when the still unconsolidated Moabite tribes had gone as far north as they dared but too far to effectively defend their northern posts. Sihon, the Amorite king, pushed southward. First he reconquered Heshbon, which was no strenuous task since it was the most northerly of the Moabite settlements. From Heshbon, the city of Sihon, a fire went out consuming Moabite cities north of the Arnon. This direction of the campaign from north to south had been correctly noted by Meyer but incorrectly interpreted as a later campaign of Israel against Moab (114). Though Sihon's conquest resulted in a temporary setback for the Moabite settlement of the area north of the Arnon, the Amorite king did not wipe out the settlement (115). Indeed, the locality of Balaam's activity, the name "plain of Moab" and the region where Moses was buried all indicate continued settlement of unoccupied areas among the cities controlled by the Amorites (115-117). The period from the defeat by Sihon to the arrival of Israel was utilized to consolidate the Moabite tribes and build fortified cities (118).

The fact that Israel after their arrival did not try to occupy Moab convinced the Moabites that the Israelites were aiming only for the territory west of the Jordan and could be trusted as allies in the struggle against the Amorites. Such fond Moabite expectations, however, were dashed after the Israelites conquered Sihon at Jahaz and chanted the song of mockery with which the Amorites had previously triumphed over Moab (119-21). This mocking song was more that just an Israelite celebration of victory over the Amorites, for it demonstrated that the Israelites were able to subjugate the Moabites just as the Amorites had done not long before (120).

As a number of Israelites saw that the conquered territory was suitable for cattle raising, they made their claim to the right of ownership by singing the "song of the well" (Num 21:16-18). This took place at Beer, from which location Jazer and Og of Bashan were conquered. No longer did the Moabites doubt that Israel had come to stay, and it was this conviction which precipitated Balak's invitation to Balaam to come and curse Israel (121-125).

Like Ewald, Van Zyl sets Num 21:21-31 in the period of the conquest, but unlike Ewald he places the events of the poem in the time prior to Israel's arrival on the borders of Moab. Knobel (cited by Gray 1903:

300), Holzinger, Maisler, Edelkoort, and Nordtzij (cited by Van Zyl 1960: 10; Hanson 1968: 293; Ottosson 1969: 62) had anticipated Van Zyl in regarding the poem an Amorite mocking song sung by their poets over the Moabite defeat; however, some of these authors suggested that the present context has modified the poem's meaning (so also Snaith 1969: 174). More recently Hanson (1968: 291-320), F. L. Moriarty (1968: 94) and H. Gilead (1977: 12-17 cited in *OTA* 1978: 248) argued that the poem originally dealt with Sihon's conquest of Moab. Van Zyl's reasons for his interpretation are that (1) different localities are given in the prose and poetic accounts for the recorded battles suggesting two different historical contexts; (2) the southward movement of the poetic account distinguishes it from the northward thrust in the prose narrative; and (3) the explanation neither requires any immediate inherent alteration of the text nor is it in conflict with the immediate historical context. Though Van Zyl does not respond to the charge of metric irregularity in Num 21:29d, possibly reads too much into the significance of the "song of the well" and brings a touch of imagination to his reconstruction of events, it must be admitted that it raises fewer problems than the alternate theories so far discussed. His interpretation commends itself, as it obviates the emphatic antitheses implied in the supposition that the poem is an Israelite satirical ode and makes redundant elaborate reconstructions which, holding the text suspect, are based largely on intuition and conjecture.

In contrast to both the traditional view of the conquest of Palestine and the concept of a peaceful infiltration, G. Mendenhall offered an interesting historical and social reconstruction (1962: 66-87). Bright followed Mendenhall's suggestion in the second edition of his *History of Israel* (1972: 133-134). While neither entered into a detailed exegesis of the Sihon story, both affirmed the conquest setting for the Heshbon account.[8]

Mendenhall recommends that

since the victory of Sihon must have taken place some time before the appearance of Israel on the scene, the most likely explanation for the inclusion of the poem in Israelite tradition is the assumption that the event celebrated involved the interests of the group who preserved it (1962: 81).

He suggests that Amorite military adventurers had come down from Syria and subjugated the population which consisted mainly of "Hebrew" farmers and shepherds who immigrated to the Transjordan from western Palestine. As these "Hebrews" had little love for "their" king and the military clique surrounding Sihon, they not only deserted him and welcomed the intruding Israelites but became Israelites themselves. Having dealt with Sihon, the Israelites were left in possession of the best of the land between the Arnon and Jabbok.

It is obvious that both Mendenhall and Bright bring a sensitive historical intuition to this narrative. Few would question that the Israelites coming from the desert were joined by peoples who had previously settled in Palestine. Similarly, Mendenhall's inference is a feasible explanation of how an Amorite taunt song could have been included in Israelite tradition. Nevertheless, Mendenhall's assumptions must remain tentative until checked by further research, particularly in the light of alternate, equally feasible explanations of the song of Heshbon.

The first scholarly article focusing on the Heshbon story, *particularly* the song of Heshbon, was published in 1968 by P. D. Hanson (291-320). Heretofore, study of the Heshbon accounts had been incidental to other interests. Hanson sought to unlock the meaning of the song by analyzing Num 21:30. This *crux interpretum* he believes became severely corrupted in the course of textual transmission. Like Van Zyl he rejects the two major lines of past scholarly interpretation of the poem embodied in the views of Ewald and Meyer. Hanson contends that the poem is the work of an Amorite poet celebrating his people's and Sihon's victory over the Moabites. The song, he maintains, was still considered an Amorite composition by the Elohist who included it in his narrative as a sort of documentary fact substantiating Sihon's prior conquest of Moabite king and land (293). This historical fact, Hanson believes, was obscured in the course of textual transmission through two scribal errors and several textual corruptions in vs. 30. As a result, the poem was ultimately applied to Israel's victory over Sihon mentioned in vss. 23 and 24 (310).

Hanson claims that

when the necessary textual emendations are made, and the provisional attempt is made to reconstruct the Song in pre-tenth-century Canaanite orthography and vocalization, a vivid, self-contained poetic unit emerges, with a very regular meter and a well balanced Canaanite poetic structure (293).

He admits that such a reconstruction must remain an experiment because the language spoken by the Amorite conquerors can be only a hypothetical extrapolation from other dialects of roughly the same period and general geographical area.

The proposed reconstruction results in a neat and regular poem of seven bicola with a seven-syllable, three-stress line in which several of the most common Canaanite parallel patterns are found (307). Cola which are considered too short or too long are adjusted to fit the suggested scansion (*e.g.* in vs. 29a "king of" is added because the colon is metrically short, while "Amorite king" is deleted in vs. 29d because it "represents the type of explanatory note that a later hand would feel prompted to add" [303]).

To reestablish vs. 30, on which there is no consensus among both ancient and modern translators and commentators, Hanson turns to conjectural emendation, haplography and readings of the Targumim and Vulgate. In this way he achieves a pair of bicola with

regular meter, parallel structure and a meaning which could form a suitable conclusion to the song and a reading which would also explain the text of the underlying versions (306). Hanson's reconstruction of vs. 30 reads:

The dominion of Moab has perished
From Heshbon as far as Dibon!
Deserted are the high places of Chemosh
From Nophah as far as Medeba!

This song is then utilized by Hanson as an historical source for the events in the Transjordanian area during the preconquest and conquest periods. The historical steps follow Van Zyl's theory closely, though less elaborately. The Moabites are said to have pushed north across the Arnon to Heshbon, subjugating the earlier settlers, until they clashed with the Amorites, who under their commander Sihon initially took the northernmost Moabite city Heshbon. Having made Heshbon his capital, Sihon then pushed south, simultaneously freeing subjugated Amorites and vanquishing Moabite cities including Dibon, Nophah, and Madaba. The poem then celebrates the rebuilding of Heshbon, the city's establishment as Sihon's capital, and the thrust against the Moabites south of Heshbon. Hanson believes that the song was later adopted by Israel's oral tradition and used by the tribes east of the Jordan as a counterclaim to Moabite demands and evidence for the fact that Israel had respected Moabite territorial rights.

Hanson's "all too free emendation" (Weippert 1979: 21) of vs. 30 has failed to attract adherents, and his scansion of the poem appears just a little too artificial. The question should also be raised whether the song would have actually been preserved in writing in Amorite. In some ways Hanson must also be charged with begging the question regarding both the national origin and date of the poem. Nevertheless, his work must be strongly commended in that it seeks some external control in order to check more objectively the probable date and historical context of the poem. His detailed effort to compare Num 21:27-30 with other early poetry and orthography had not been explored before and though it lacks refinement it certainly seems to point in the right direction. Indeed, such a comparison with ancient poetry could offer a badly needed external control (provided the poetry is archaic and not merely archaizing), supplying an anchor for the analysis of the Heshbon tradition, which so far has drifted somewhat aimlessly on the sea of divergent scholarly opinions.

Hanson's study argues for a possible antiquity of the song, a suggestion which recommends itself because it is in harmony with the combined witness of the biblical tradition which places Sihon in the context of the conquest.

More recently Hanson's basic approach was followed by D. K. Stuart (1976: 93-95, 33). Stuart cast the song in an early Israelite orthography and in an analysis of early Hebrew and Ugaritic poetry concluded that "this short song exhibits several interesting features including metrical regularity, balanced couplets, rhyme (vss. 27, 28), mixed meter, a triplet, and indications of very archaic orthography" (93).

In his reconstruction of the song Stuart incorporates a number of textual emendations suggested by Hanson though he considers vs. 30 as too corrupt to present confidently in the text. With Freedman he rejects Hanson's rather forced 7:7 scansion of each couplet and contends that the meter is mixed. This judgment appears more likely, as does also Stuart's suggestion that vs. 29 is a combination of a 6:6 couplet and a 7:7:7 tricolon which incorporates as integral the phrase "to the king of the Amorites, Sihon" (93). Perhaps Stuart's repeated cautions against the temptation to emend the poetic text too readily should be taken seriously, particularly in the light of more recent studies of early Hebrew and Canaanite poetry which have demonstrated that a number of emendations proposed by earlier scholars were largely subjective and premature (cf. 215-217).

In the same year that Hanson's study appeared, W. A. Sumner examined the Sihon tradition in the larger context of research into Israel's encounter with the five nations east of the Jordan recorded in Deut 2:1-3, 11 (1968: 216-228). Sumner noted that the account of each nation (Edom, Moab, Ammon, Sihon and Og) conforms to a literary "pattern and contains the same or equivalent elements, which are often expressed in the same words" (216). There are five major elements which Sumner argues recur in all five accounts: (1) the movement, (2) Yahweh's instructions, (3) the prehistory of each settlement, (4) the provision of food, and (5) the departure or occupation (218). The structure and antitheses of two peaceful encounters balanced by two warlike encounters (the story of Ammon is an odd encounter placed between the passages which show the change in circumstances and policy) are an artificial literary device, the gist of which the Deuteronomist has already found in his sources (217, 222-23).

His analysis of Deut 2:1-3, 11 Sumner finds corroborated in Num 20-21. In Numbers the author grouped Israel's dealings with Edom (20:14-21) and Sihon (21:21-31) similarly to achieve a balance between one peaceful and one warlike account. While Sumner thinks it likely that the Numbers accounts (belonging to E) antedate Deut 2:1-3, 11 he doubts that the latter is dependent upon the former. Instead, both are thought to have utilized more ancient traditions which contained not only the balance between peaceful and warlike encounters but also the five elements listed above (226-27).

Few would doubt that Numbers and Deuteronomy utilize more ancient traditions, and many would affirm that Deuteronomy arranges and structures the earlier materials, giving them a theological interpretation. However, several considerations would put Sumner's proposed literary balance and structure in question. The pattern and balance cannot be achieved without some significant and unjustified sacrifices. Not only is

the Ammon story an odd one out in Deut 2 but the Og account, which is essential to the balance of two warlike and two peaceful encounters in Deuteronomy, has to be dispensed with in Numbers because there it upsets the balance of one peaceful and one warlike encounter. Sumner admits that there is a significant distance which separates the Edom and Sihon stories in Numbers but thinks that the "strong literary connection between them more than compensates for this" (125). This, however, appears to beg the question. While Sumner allows for some minor modifications, it is clear that in several cases the five individual elements which he has singled out do not appear in all five accounts. Since, however, Sumner's theory of literary relations depends largely on the repetition of these elements in the accounts, he can only sustain his hypothesis by assuming what he is trying to prove (cf. Coats 1976: 186 n. 29). All of this puts in doubt not only the proposed artistically devised structure and balance as an artificial literary device, but also the precise content and form of the earlier traditions.

M. Ottosson's discussion of the Sihon story (1969: 53-73) leans somewhat on Sumner's paper. He embarks upon his study by noting the similarities between the Jacob/Israel and Esau/Edom narrative of Gen 33, the encounter of Israel and Edom in Num 20, and the Sihon account in Num 21:21-31 within the larger context of the inheritance theme. Ottosson believes that the main trend of Num 21 is Israel's peaceful intentions (except toward Sihon) shown in her respect for her neighbors' rights of inheritance (57).

Like Noth, Ottosson accepts the literary unity of Num 21:21-31 but attributes it to a predeuteronomistic P-traditionist. He believes the narrative account reflects an Israelite battle against the Amorites who had previously wrested the land from the Moabites. This victory over Sihon (Ottosson accepts the integrity of vs. 29d "to the Amorite king Sihon" [66]) confirmed Israel's hereditary right to the area between the Arnon and the Jabbok (57).

Ottosson lists three alternative explanations for the song of Heshbon. He rejects Ewald's interpretation but is attracted to the view that this is an Amorite *māšāl* quoted against Moab. However, if we understand Ottosson aright, he prefers a third alternative which considers the poem a representation of an Israelite struggle with Moab for the country of Sihon (62-66). He renders the verbs of vs. 28 and the woe-saying in vs. 29a by futures and thinks these passages express Israelite belligerence to Moab as the former look toward the events expressed in Num 22-24. The mood changes in vs. 29b. *Nāthān* introducing vs. 29b is translated by a perfect; the verse is said to refer to Moab's defeat at the hands of Sihon. Though Ottosson also sees vs. 30 as problematical, he links it with vs. 29b-d and contends that it reflects Moab's defeat by Sihon.

Seen in the light of Israel's claim to an inheritance north of the Arnon the verse explains that all these places were wrested from Moab by the

Amorites, so that Israel believed she had every right to defy the claims of the neighbour peoples, *cf*. Jg. 11 vv 12ff. (67 n. 52).

In sum, Ottosson places the context of Num 21:21-31 in the conquest period and regards it as reflective of Israel's defeat of Sihon and Israel's future belligerence towards Moab as depicted in Num 22-24. The latter suggestion, while novel and intriguing, depends entirely on the propriety of Ottosson's translation of the *tempora*. Actually, there is hardly any justification for rendering the perfects by future tenses in vss. 28-29a but by preterites beginning with 29b apart from the relation Ottosson presupposes between Num 21:28-29 and chaps. 22-24.

One year after Hanson's essay on the Heshbon poem had been published, J. R. Bartlett's analysis of the song appeared (1969: 94-100). Presumably, Bartlett had not had access to Hanson's work as he makes no reference to it. He dismisses the interpretation of the poem advanced by Ewald and Noth because in his estimate vss. 28-29 refer to the same campaign or wave of destruction as vs. 30 (1969: 97). Though Bartlett reflects the Omride historical context of the poem, he aligns himself with the interpretations offered by Meyer and Stade (96-100). Bartlett divests the poem from the putative Amorite situation and searches the biblical traditions for a period during which the country of Moab not only extended north of the Arnon, but also when the original interest of the poem (which he attributes to E) had become confused enough to be understood apart from Sihon. Though he admits that there is "no strong supporting evidence" (100), Bartlett decides that the harsh campaign of David against Moab recorded in 2 Sam 8:2, 12 could have given rise to Num 21:27-30 as a mocking or victory song which originated at David's court:

> In short, we may tentatively suggest that the song of Num. 21:27b-30 comes from the tenth century B.C., probably from Jerusalem, and had reference to the campaign of David against Moab. This allows time for the Moabites to have extended their territory north of the Arnon, and time for the original reference of the song to have become obscure to the narrator of Num. 21, who may have drawn false conclusions from the reference in the song to 'the city of Sihon'. But until we can agree upon the correct text and translation of these difficult verses, it is unlikely that we shall be able to agree upon the original historical event which lies behind them (1969: 100).

Bartlett is led to his conclusions by stating three objections to the interpretations which locate the poem in the conquest period (1969: 94-95). Two of these objections had been anticipated by Meyer (1881: 130-131). They are the claim that the poem describes a north-to-south thrust and the postulate that vs. 29d overburdens the meter of the poem. Once we dispense with the Sihon clause in vs. 29d, the poem is freed from the historical moorings of antiquity and may be docked to any seemingly appropriate historical situation. Bartlett further objects that we cannot be certain whether Heshbon, Madaba (probably also Nophah), and Dibon were in Moabite hands during the 13th century B.C. Furthermore, the consistent biblical tradition assumes that the predecessors of the tribes Reuben and Gad were Amorites and not Moabites. From this, Bartlett infers that any references to cities under Moabite denomination during the conquest period would be anachronistic.

While Bartlett correctly draws attention to the southward movement of the poem, this is not contrary to an Amorite thrust against Moab before the Israelite conquest. The meter of Num 21:29d appears to present a problem in the larger context of the poem primarily because of our commitment to somewhat antiquated and inflexible canons of meter and scansion which have to be modified considerably in the light of recent analyses of early Hebrew and Ugaritic poetry (*cf*. Cross and Freedman 1952, 1975; Stuart 1976).

Though there is sufficient data to cast suspicion upon the text of vs. 30, there is not the slightest textual evidence that vs. 29d was ever corrupt or held suspect. Indeed, echoes of the phrase "to the Amorite king Sihon" elsewhere in both the poem (*e.g*. vss. 27, 28) and the accompanying narrative (vss. 21, 23, 26) provide evidence that the phrase is embedded in and integral to the story. The removal of this phrase would have to be followed by an erasure of its traces in the poem and narrative, denuding the story significantly of its impact. Alternate theories which have been achieved at considerable expense and doubtful reconstruction reduce this story to the level of the lame and somewhat trite. No support for the omission of this more difficult reading can be substantiated by the use of parts of this poem in Jer 48:45-47. It is evident from the remainder of Jer 48 that older fragments were used throughout. Futhermore Jeremiah cites Num 21:27-30 selectively and utilizes it creatively in the context of the oracle against Moab (we will return to Jer 48 below). Finally, a considerable number of critics—though not on the basis of the latest research into poetic scansion—have seen no major problems in retaining the reading of vs. 29d either in part or in whole.

Bartlett's third argument, that the evidence for Moabite control of the land north of the Arnon in the 13th century is weak, is most surprising (94-95). The objection is based primarily on an *argumentum e silentio* and rejection of the witness of vs. 26. The latter is believed to have derived its data from the poem, which Bartlett in turn regards as unhistorical.

We noted above that the north-to-south movement of the poem is at least compatible with an Amorite thrust before the conquest. We also have seen no decisive reason for doubting the reading in vs. 29d which places the poem in this early period. In the light of this we need impugn neither the poem nor vs. 26 as a witness for the Moabite control of the area north of the Arnon during this early period. What is puzzling, however, is the fact that Bartlett cites no external sources which disclaim Moabite control over this area of Transjordan in the conquest period. The best he can do is to note that there are no external sources which claim control over the region. Surely, this is hardly valid when, as Weippert observes regarding the Transjordan during the end of the Late Bronze Age and the beginning of the Iron Age, "we do not yet have a clear picture of this period of transition" (1979: 25; cf. 26-30). In the light of the archaeological survey of Central Moab we will await the results of similar surveys of the area north of the Arnon (Miller 1979: 43-52; Kautz 1981: 27-35). Until more evidence surfaces, Weippert's remark should act as a caveat against basing too much on an argument from silence. Equally, Bartlett's observation that the consistent biblical tradition describes Amorites and not Moabites as Israel's predecessors in the region is precisely what we would expect on the basis of information provided in Num 21:21-31. Had the sources indicated what Bartlett infers we would have had serious reasons for suspicion. As the tradition stands, it depicts a Moabite settlement conquered by Amorites who in turn were dealt with by the Israelites.

These considerations tend to seriously undermine the plausibility of Bartlett's hypothesis regarding the meaning and significance of Num 21:27-30. Bartlett's thesis becomes even more doubtful when we examine the passage in 2 Sam 8:2, 12 which he alleges may provide the historical situation for the poem of Heshbon. 2 Sam 8:2 tells us only that David defeated the Moabites and then executed a third of the force which he had compelled to lie on the ground. There is not the slightest hint or contact between this story and the Heshbon account. If it be alleged that the story was radically transformed, then we must admit that we have no methodological reference point to make any historical decision. Such skepticism, however, seems hardly called for in the case of an account which etched itself so deeply upon the historical memory of Israel. Likewise, it is extremely doubtful that this story was forgotten so soon and misunderstood so completely when the detailed witness of the Sihon account remained rather stable and consistent in Israel's tradition. The story (and the poem) recounted in Num 21:21-31 is neither improbable in itself, nor inconsistent with the general account repeated in the later Sihon testimonies nor is it likely to have been invented. In fact, Smith observed that there was nothing to be gained by inventing the account (n.d.: 663).

One year after Bartlett's views on the poem of Heshbon appeared, he published a traditio-historical study of the Sihon tradition (1970: 257-277). Though based on Noth's earlier research, Bartlett endeavored to extend his work by developing a hypothesis which seeks to explain how the Transjordanian tradition ultimately reached Jerusalem or Samaria and give reasons for its preservation (1970: 257). Relying on Noth,

Bartlett supposes that the Deuteronomic description of Sihon's kingdom extending from the Arnon to the Jabbok is merely the end product of a long and complex history of tradition (258, 276) in which the compiler of the Deuteronomic tradition simplified the division of the Transjordan into two parts and artificially widened an originally smaller kingdom of Sihon limited to the tableland stretching southward from Heshbon to the wādī eth-thamad (261). Bartlett further postulates that the stories of Sihon and Og originally belonged to different peoples, places, and periods (268) and only later in the exilic Israelite tradition did these kings come to be known as fellow Amorites, neighbors, and contemporaries. More specifically, Bartlett suggests that the Jairites by virtue of their geographical proximity to the region of Bashan were ultimately responsible for the traditions concerning a battle of Og with the Israelites (271). Though contrary to R. de Vaux, Bartlett sees some historicity in the battle of Edrei (267, 271), he does not tell us what really happened except to make this link with the Jairites.

Bartlett adds that since the "land of Sihon became Gadite territory" (272), the Sihon tradition must have passed into the larger Israelite literary blood stream of the Elohist source through the Gadites via traditions of the north (272).

The clans Jair and Gad then communicated these traditions about Sihon and Og, preserved in oral form, through the liturgy (cf. Ps 135:11; 136:19-20) at the sanctuary in Gilgal. It is from here that the Elohist source and Deuteronomy drew their stories of the two kings (273-275). In Deuteronomy, as part of the Deuteronomist scheme, which presents the story of occupation and settlement in Transjordan in terms of a simple division of the land into two parts, the territories of Sihon and Og were made to appear much greater than they actually had been (276).

Though Bartlett's rather creative study proceeds with considerable caution (271-273), his thesis is not without problems. Undoubtedly the history of the settlement east of the Jordan was complex and it is not inconceivable that the Jairites, Gadites and the cult contributed to keeping the Og and Sihon traditions alive. Yet Bartlett's theory suffers from the serious disadvantage that it is beyond verification and rests too much on possibilities (271-273). For this reason the central core of his reconstruction is of limited value unless the proposed initial and final stages of his traditio-historical development are sufficiently convincing to commend the probability of his theory.

Since Bartlett attaches greater significance to the first stage of the proposed growth of the geographical extent of Sihon's kingdom, we will leave its evaluation till later. His claim that the extent of Sihon's kingdom from Arnon to Jabbok and the bifurcation of Gilead represents the last stage of the development presupposes a reasonably clear progression from a threefold to a twofold division of the Transjordan. It is strange then that the earliest evidence for the tripartite division is found in Deut 3:10. Furthermore, this threefold conception of the land into tableland, Gilead, and Bashan is retained for the cities of refuge in Deut 4:43 and Josh 20:8 (other references to the tripartite arrangement in Deuteronomy-Joshua are in Josh 13:9, 16, 17, 21). On the other hand, the twofold division of the Transjordan which *ex hypothesi* we would expect *de novo* in Deuteronomy-Joshua occurs first in the present canonical order in Num 21:24 (*cf.* the implications of a twofold order in Num 32) and very rarely in Deuteronomy-Joshua (*cf.* Deut 3:8, Josh 13:5). Though the value of the testimonies recorded in Num 21 and 32 depends largely on our critical dating of these materials, it is clear that the biblical data are completely silent as to when—if indeed ever—such a deliberate division into the alleged twofold scheme took place. While it is not inconceivable that the extent of Sihon's kingdom and the subsequent division of the Transjordan among the tribes of Reuben, Gad and half-Manasseh precipitated the halving of Gilead and the area east of the Jordan, it seems that both the twofold and threefold forms of land division were employed in the testimonies of Deuteronomy-Joshua as alternate but contemporaneous partitions of this area. This, however, would invalidate the use of the alleged twofold division as merely the last traditio-historical stage in our analysis of the Sihon tradition.

Though the last of Bartlett's traditio-historical stages is not too compelling, it must be said that he rests his case on an analysis of the first stage of the traditio-historical development (258). Accordingly, he suggests that Sihon's kingdom was really limited to the tableland stretching southward from Heshbon to the *wādī eth-thamad* (261).

Bartlett's evidence is (1) a dismissal of the geographical information provided by the song of Num 21:27-30 because he attributes its historical context to the time of David, as we noted above; (2) an identification of Jahaz as the southernmost border of Sihon's kingdom; and (3) an interpretation of Num 32:1 which regards Sihon's kingdom as bounded by Jazer and Gilead in the north.

However, we have already noted that Bartlett's interpretation of the poem is hardly warranted. Hence we are not justified in dismissing the poem's geographical information, which is in harmony with unimpeached passages citing the Arnon as the earliest Moabite boundary (*e.g.* Num 21:13-15, 22:36; Deut 2:18; Judg 11:18, 22).

Bartlett identifies Jahaz with *el-medieyineh* (259, 261) and considers this location to have been Sihon's southernmost border. This argument is untenable because the location of Jahaz is still a matter of considerable dispute and according to Num 21 was only the site of the military engagement between the Israelites and Sihon. While generally a battlefield may or may not be on the border, there is nothing in the tradition which indicates that Jahaz should be understood as a border post.

Similarly, Bartlett's interpretation of Num 32:1 appears rather forced. While the rather terse account of Jazer's conquest (Num 21:32) is distinct from the battle with the king of Heshbon and may therefore indicate a location outside of Sihon's jurisdiction, it would be assuming too much to locate Gilead wholly outside of the borders of Sihon's realm merely on the basis of Num 32:1 (*cf.* Aharoni 1967: 80, 276).

Though much depends on one's definition of tradition-criticism, it seems that the arguments advanced by Bartlett for the first and last stages of the tradition's growth do not square with the evidence. Indeed, from a methodological viewpoint we would expect far greater tensions to warrant his proposed growth pattern. Certainly the criteria advanced seem inadequate to develop his elaborate synthesis from a beginning clearly recognizable oral stage to the larger literary units.

The stress on primitive oral traditions behind the episodes recorded in the Pentateuchal narratives in the context of the traditio-historical methodology was attacked by J. Van Seters in 1972 (182-197). His significant analysis of the Sihon conquest aimed at demonstrating a greater literary dependence of the conquest stories. Van Seters argued that

> such questions of tradition history cannot be discussed until the literary character of the text is more fully clarified. The possibility must be considered that the text is a literary creation or a 'redactional' development of earlier literary works, in which case any discussion of oral tradition would be immensely complicated (182; *cf.* 197).

Van Seters concludes that the oldest accounts of the literary tradition depicting the conquest of the kingdom of Sihon and Og are the

> rather late deuteronomistic ones and they have a highly ideological character which make these episodes historically untrustworthy. In the area of literary criticism we are faced with the possibility of a post-deuteronomic body of literature in the Pentateuch distinct from 'P' in the so-called JE corpus (how extensive remains to be discovered) which seems to be at least partly redactional of earlier literary levels of the tradition. . . . The possibility of a literary 'artificial' development of the tradition without any great antiquity must be seriously considered (197).

Van Seters decides that only a literary dependence can account for the numerous verbal parallels in Num 21:21-25; Deut 2:26-37 and Judg 11:19-26 (184-186). Furthermore, since the wording of Numbers often agrees closely with that of Judges and the story in Numbers and Judges differs in the same way from Deuteronomy (186), Numbers "must be dependent upon Judges and not vice versa" (187).

Van Seters' judgment appears confirmed by the form-critical analysis of the battle report by W. Richter

(1966: 262-264). Against J. G. Plöger's suggestion that the *Sitz im Leben* of the *Kampfbericht* (Plöger depends more heavily on references in Deuteronomy and Joshua) is in the ancient amphictyonic institution of the Holy War, Van Seters looks to the Assyrian annals and Neo-Babylonian chronicles for the historical situation of this form. He contends that the Assyrian commemorative inscription parallels the Deut 2 account of Sihon while the Num 21 story finds a correspondence in the Neo-Babylonian chronicle. In the former genre the exploits of the king and the assistance of the deity are noted, he claims, while the latter lacks or at least very rarely records the element of divine intervention. This parallel of forms then dates the Numbers account after that in Deuteronomy to the exilic period (187-189).

Further support for the priority of Deuteronomy and Judges is derived from the rather "unsuccessful" conflation of readings from Deuteronomy and Judges in Numbers and the alleged dependence of Num 20:17-19 (of which the messenger speech in Num 21:22 is considered to be a shorter version in the same hand) on Deut 2:27-29 (189-191). The writer-redactor built up the narrative of Num 21:21-31 by utilizing deuteronomic sources such as Deut 2:26-37 and Judg 11:19-26 for vss. 21-25 and then borrowing a taunt song against Moab, vss. 27-30 which was reworked and fitted into the account with transition passages vss., 26, 31 (195).

Van Seters agrees with Meyer (1881: 117-146) that the poem is not about Israel's conquest of Sihon (1972: 195, 1980: 117-118). He thinks the song was included in Num 21:21-31 simply because of its reference to Sihon. The author responsible for this inclusion then sought to make the reference to Sihon more direct by adding "to the king of the Amorites, Sihon" in vs. 29d, a phrase which according to Van Seters over-balances the line and is not found in Jer 48:45-47 (1972: 195). Van Seters claims that Num 21:27-30 and Jer 48:45-47 actually go back to a common *Vorlage* and thinks that the poem had its origin in an exilic collection of taunt songs within the larger context of oracles against the nations (specifically Moab). He adds: "This picture of Heshbon as destroyed along with other Moabite cities is presented in a number of other closely related oracles in Isaiah 15-16 and Jeremiah 48" (194). In conclusion, "the account in Numbers is post-deuteronomic and must be regarded as late-exilic at the earliest" (196). Consequently,

> On the historical level the conquest of the kingdoms of Sihon and Og must be regarded with grave suspicion. The oldest accounts in the literary tradition are the rather late deuteronomistic ones and they have a highly ideological character which make these episodes historically untrustworthy (197).

Van Seters' literary examination of the conquest of Sihon's kingdom is unique, stimulating and thorough. He is the first to analyze comprehensively the Sihon conquest in Numbers, Deuteronomy, Judges, and Jeremiah. He scrutinizes the poem in the light of Jer 48 as did Meyer (1881: 131). Like Hanson he must be commended for seeking some external control to date his literary reconstruction, for which purpose he, however, turns to Assyrian annals and Neo-Babylonian documents.

Nevertheless, Van Seters' hypothesis has not gone unchallenged (Gunn 1974: 513-518; Coats 1976: 182; Bartlett 1978: 347-351. Van Seters published a response to Gunn in 1976 [139-154]). While Bartlett limited himself to a consideration of the relationship of Num 21:21-25 to Deuteronomy and Judges and Van Seters finds fault with some of Bartlett's objections (1980: 117-119), much of Bartlett's thrust against the dependence of Numbers on Judges and Deuteronomy has not been adequately answered. Van Seters had argued that the reading "Israel" instead of "Moses" in Num 21:21 and the settlement of the Israelites in Num 21:24-25 were appropriate in the context of Judg 11 but a "striking inconsistency" and a "false conclusion" in Numbers (186). Hence the Numbers account must be later than Judg 11.

Bartlett correctly responded:

> If the Numbers editor of the Sihon story derived the use of 'Israel' from Judges 11, then he seems to have extended this use (on Van Seters' hypothesis) to a number of other stories between Num 20:14 and 25:6. It seems more likely, however, that Judges 11 drew on the wide range of material available to him in Numbers than that Numbers drew on Judges 11 and extended the use of 'Israel' in this way to other stories relating to this wilderness period (1978: 348).

Van Seters' response (1980: 117) that Bartlett's objection misses the point at issue, which is "the specific use of Israel in 21:21 in place of Moses" will not stand, for the context is as important here as elsewhere where Van Seters insists on the broader setting. To this one could add that though "Moses" rather than "Israel" might be expected in vs. 21, similar variations between representative leader and people are evident elsewhere in Numbers (*e.g.* Israel/Moses and Edom/king of Edom [Num 20:14-21] and Moab/Balak [Num 22:1-14]); hence the reading of vs. 21 is in keeping with the larger context.

Again it is true that the reference to Israel's settlement in Heshbon and its villages (*i.e.* its dependencies) is difficult in the light of subsequent episodes on settlement (*e.g.* Num 32:1-2). Nevertheless to call this a "false conclusion" is excessive language. Bartlett prefers to call this an "anticipatory conclusion" and thinks it might

> equally well have arisen from the juxtaposition in Numbers of the Sihon story and its result with the material about the settlement of Reuben and Gad. ... The explanation we adopt of the 'false conclusion' depends upon our view of the literary history of the passage, and cannot be a

basic plank of Van Seters' reconstruction (1978: 349).

Surely the temporal relation between the event and its record is crucial and vs. 25 may reflect no more than a recording of Israel's settlement after the event of settlement. The statement may be understood as either an "anticipatory conclusion" or a broad "summary conclusion" registered after Israel (*i.e.*, part thereof) settled in the area.

The argument that Numbers conflates the references to captured territory from Judg 11:21-22 and to "these cities" from Deut 2:34 is also doubtful (1972: 189). If, as Van Seters argues (1980: 117), Deut 2:31 is a reference back to Num 21:24, then it seems far more likely that Deut 2:31, 36-37 is an elaboration of both the captured territory and cities referred to in Num 21. Incidentally, the clause "and Israel took all these cities" may not be as abrupt as has at times been assumed when it is remembered that the demonstrative pronoun *ʾelleh* may also have grammatical relations to what follows and need not refer only to preceding items.

These considerations call into question the alleged dependence of Numbers on Judges. Application of tests for priority and dependence standard in synoptic criticism appear to further assail the dependence of Numbers on Judges and Deuteronomy. Van Seters repeatedly draws attention to distinct similarities between the redactional literary process of the Sihon conquest passages and that of the synoptic gospels (1972: 184, 197). Though he comments that it would be useful in all such cases of parallel passages to apply the same basic tests, he unfortunately does not spell out which criteria OT critics should adopt from their colleagues in synoptic criticism, which itself is experiencing a period of reassessment. We presume that Van Seters refers to the traditional tests of wording, content, order, etc.[9]

While this is not the place to enter into a prolonged discussion of these tests, a brief and somewhat limited application of the criteria of content and order to the Sihon materials may be justified.

A comparison of the three sources makes it evident that the content of Num 21:21-25 is found almost *in toto* in both Deuteronomy and Judges. Numbers is certainly more compact than either Deuteronomy or Judges. Deuteronomy 2, cast in the language of a first-person speech of Moses, tends to be expansionist, especially as it repeatedly notes divine intervention (*e.g.* 2:29, 31, 33, 36, 37). Similarly, Judg 11 contains a number of statements reflecting divine intervention (vss. 21, 23, 24) which are completely absent from Num 21:21-25. Surely we could have expected this extremely significant element characterizing divine aid in Num 21 had it been a conflation of Deut 2 and Judg 11.

Again the relative order of the three narratives tends to support the priority of Num 21. The order of Num 21 is generally supported by both Deuteronomy and Judges and wherever either departs from Numbers the other usually maintains the order. Indeed, after a

deviation from Numbers both Deut 2 and Judg 11 return to the same basic outline of Numbers. For example, after the request to purchase food and drink (Deut 2:28-29, not in Judg 11) Deuteronomy expands and departs from Num 21:22 only to return to the order of Numbers and Judges in listing Sihon's refusal to let Israel pass (Num 21:23a; Deut 2:30; Judg 11:20). Following Sihon's rebuttal, Deut 2:30b-31 again diverges from Numbers as it notes Yahweh's hardening of Sihon's heart and his promise to give Sihon over to Israel. Deuteronomy 2:32 then returns to the narrative of Num 21:23b, reporting the battle at Jahaz (*cf.* Judg 11:20) before departing from Numbers in company with Judg 11:21 to observe the divine intervention. Both Deut 2:33a and Judg 11:21b revert to Num 21:24 stating Sihon's defeat. After a recital of persons slain and territory captured (which Deut 2:34, 35 expands) both Deut 2:36b and Judg 11:23a attribute the victory to divine providence. Numbers 21:26-30 then supplies unique information concerning Heshbon's prehistory.

This, albeit too brief, investigation tends to argue for the priority of Num 21:21-25, with later expansions in Deut 2, and a résumé conflating Numbers and Deuteronomy in Judg 11. Bartlett's assessment of this order seems to be supported:

> Jephthah's speech in Judg 11:14-26 contains what seems to be a résumé of fuller material (compare, for example, Judg 11:19-23 with the longer, more detailed account of Num 21:21-31, and note the brief allusion to the story of Balak in Judg 11:25). If the Numbers account is based on Judg 11 and Deuteronomy, then we shall have to find a new source for all the material in Numbers which does not appear in Judg 11 or Deuteronomy (348).

Another criticism of Van Seters' theory relates to his use of form-criticism. He claims that of the forms in which military conquests were recorded in the ANE Num 21 comes closest to the Neo-Babylonian chronicle. This form-critical assessment leads him to attribute a post-deuteronomic late-exilic date to Num 21:21-25 (1972: 196). However, Van Seters admits correctly that the extrabiblical accounts are much more elaborate and verbose than the alleged biblical counterpart (1972: 188). Furthermore, while the parallels amount to no more than might be expected in any battle report, there is a great deal of matter which remains unparalleled. Both Richter (1966: 262-264) and Van Seters generalize too freely and provide extremely loose definitions (see Gunn 1974: 517-518). Indeed, their definition is so broad that it can be applied to such widely separated texts as the Neo-Babylonian chronicle and historical texts of Suppiluliuma (*cf.* ANET 318). Recently W. H. Shea argued that the predominance of chronological information and dates in the chronicle forms, so conspicuously absent from Num 21, argues further against the affinities Van Seters proposed between Num 21 and the Babylonian chronicle (1979: 8-10). These considerations tend to favor Bartlett's evaluation that "dependence of the form of the Sihon battle accounts on the Assyrian/Neo-Babylonian annalistic or chronicle forms, then, cannot be taken as proved or as determinative for dating" (1978: 350).

Van Seters challenges Bartlett for calling his arguments into question without relating to his analysis of the poem. Since Bartlett also denies the conquest setting of Num 21:27-30 (1969: 94-100), he must find himself somewhat embarrassed by Van Seters' consistent and correct claim that the poem and surrounding narrative share the same fate. Van Seters is prepared to place both into the exilic period.

His late-dating of the poem is based on the conviction that Num 21:27-30 and Jer 48:45-47 are of one cloth. This argument, however, seems to suffer from oversimplification. Jeremiah 48 is a poem or series of poems, together with a number of prose comments and expansions directed against Moab (Bright 1965: 321). The chapter contains numerous verbal similarities to various poems found elsewhere in the Bible. These include references from Isa 15-16, 24 and Num 21 and 24. Jeremiah 48:45-47, rather than reproducing Num 21:27-30, as one would expect on Van Seters' argument, includes snatches from Num 21:28a and Num 21:29 separated by a fragment from Num 24:17c. Aside from these parallels to elements from both Num 21 and 24 there is also material which is adapted or unparalleled in both Num 21 and Jer 48.

This rather discriminate use of fragments from other biblical poems in Jer 48, particularly the selection of snatches from Num 21:28-29 and 24:17 and their modification in the Jeremiah context, suggests that Jer 48:45-47 is creatively adapting older materials (*cf.* Sturdy 1976: 154). In the words of Bright:

> In the present form of the chapter [Jer 48], this older, conventional material has been adapted and supplemented and made to apply to the situation that obtained contemporaneous with the last days of Judah and just after (1965: 322).

This relationship between the song of Heshbon and Jer 48 is also supported by the fact that no decisive reasons have been advanced for rejecting the putative antiquity of Num 21:27-30.

Finally, dissatisfaction could be expressed regarding the function Van Seters attributes to this Transjordanian conquest tradition. He argues that the "promised land" motif, so prominent throughout Deuteronomy, no longer envisages the eastern region as belonging to Israel during and after the exile (1972: 196-197). If this is the case, we are left to wonder what motivated the elaborate literary artificial construct proposed by Van Seters. Indeed, we would question whether the vigorous content of the Sihon account is justified by the rather bland and lame function he attributes to it during the late exile.[10]

In sum, we would concur with Bartlett's appraisal that Van Seters has not "succeeded in showing that Num 21:21-25 is the result of the conflation of the accounts in Deut 2:26-37 and Judg 11:19-26" (1978:

351). Equally dubious is his interpretation of the song of Heshbon and the suggestion that the Heshbon tradition is an unhistorical artificial literary construct dated to the exilic period.

Recent literary criticism has strongly influenced two brief assessments of the Sihon story by J. M. Miller (1977a: 213-284 esp. 225-227, 1977b: 1-7). In a study of the Israelite occupation of Canaan, Miller's analysis of the Heshbon tradition centers primarily on Num 21:21-31 which he claims belongs essentially to the deuteronomistic stratum of the OT (1977a: 225, 227). In a response given at the Heshbon Symposium in San Francisco, Miller added that literary critics who analyzed the Sihon tradition during the past century have rarely disagreed "that the narrative materials pertaining to Sihon are thoroughly Deuteronomistic in their present form and reflect primarily theological concerns" (1977b: 2).

Not only does the narrative of Num 21:21-24a, 25 appear "to be a typically Deuteronomistic composition" (1977a: 226) but also the song in vss. 27-30, designed to justify Israel's possession of Moabite territory, is a further indication of the Deuteronomistic orientation of the passage. The reason for the latter assessment is that

> Both the idea that the lands of Edom, Moab, and Ammon were forbidden to the Israelites for a possession and the explanation that Israel received the Moabite territory in question from Sihon and the Ammonites, find their clearest expression in two clearly Deuteronomistic passages (1977a: 226).

—*i.e.* Moses' farewell address, especially Deut 2:4-5, 9, 19, and Judg 11:12-28.

The song in Num 21:27-30, Miller suggests, is an alternate version of Jer 48:45-47, and a comparison of the two passages reveals that Num 21:27-30 originally had nothing to do with a victory of Sihon over Moab. Instead the poem is an old song which commemorates an Israelite victory over Moab possibly during the reign of David. Numbers 21:26 and 31 are merely redactional verses which incorporate the song of Heshbon in its present context and the "claim that Israel gained immediate and full possession of the central and northern Transjordan by defeating Sihon and Og is probably an exaggeration or entirely fanciful" (1977a: 227). In sum,

> Analysis of the Sihon traditions in accordance with the various literary-critical methodologies have [sic] led commentators over the past century to the virtually unanimous conclusion that these traditions are historically misleading in their present form and context (1977b: 1).

Miller's position appears to be a selective composite which may be traced back particularly to views espoused by Meyer, Bartlett, and Van Seters. However, it is unfortunate that Miller rarely gives reasons for his acceptance of some of their tenets and rejection of others. He discusses the song as a testimony from the conquest period for the very reasons Meyer advanced (1881: 129-131), though Miller refuses Meyer's Omride interpretation. Similarly, Miller's explanation of vs. 26 substantially repeats Meyer. He accepts Bartlett's proposal that the song of Heshbon commemorates an Israelite victory over Moab during the reign of David, but contrary to Bartlett claims that the narrative of vss. 21-25 is a typically Deuteronomistic composition. Van Seters' stress on the extremely late and artificial literary nature of the Sihon conquest seems to have further contributed to Miller's skepticism. Miller agrees with Van Seters that the poem in Num 21:27-30 is an alternate version of Jer 48:45-47, but parts company when he detaches the song from the narrative context and attributes it to the time of David. The concern to justify Israel's possession of Moabite territory is cited as an evidence for the deuteronomistic orientation of the passage. However, this is hardly compelling, for while this motif may be explicit in Deuteronomy and Judges, it is only implicit—if that—in Numbers. If anything, the Heshbon account in Numbers may have contributed to this theological interpretation in Deuteronomy and Judges rather than vice versa.

In the light of the above critical review of the literature, Miller's assessments that (1) commentators of the past century have almost unanimously concluded that the Sihon traditions are "historically misleading in their present form and context," and (2) the narrative materials pertaining to Sihon are "thoroughly Deuteronomistic in their present form" must be adjudged as infelicitous generalizations.

Without doubt most commentators during the last hundred years agreed that the Sihon tradition was (1) reduced to writing a considerable time after the event, (2) (probably) passed on by oral tradition for some time, (3) in its present form witnesses to some redactional changes, and (4) reflected certain theological concerns. While there was disagreement on the precise source of Num 21:21-31 (the majority favored E regardless of whether they incorporated the interpretations of Ewald or Meyer), commentators agreed (with the notable exception of Van Seters) that the Numbers account preceded that of Deuteronomy and Judges.

Whereas most scholars recognized deuteronomistic touches in the Numbers tradition, Miller tends to confuse such touches with the idea that the whole tradition is primarily, if not exclusively, deuteronomistic or redactional in origin (the latter is exemplified particularly in Van Seters). Miller is right when he infers that such an evaluation reflects on the historical worth of such texts. Nevertheless, while an artificial literary construction seriously undercuts, if not completely invalidates, the historical worth of a tradition, redactional touches need not (even Noth's rather complex redactional hypothesis did not deter him from assuming a historical kernel behind the Heshbon story [1972: 73]). Though few serious commentators would deny that the Sihon traditions reflect theological concerns, such a judgment does not simultaneously impugn the historical value of a story. Methodologically, such untrustworthiness must be demonstrated on other grounds. Unfortunately, Miller has failed to recognize some of these subtle distinctions and as a result his inferences and conclusions must be treated with extreme caution.

We need not evaluate Miller's assessment of the poem, as this has already been done in the above reviews of Bartlett and Van Seters. It may be added, however, that much of the skepticism regarding the narrative is elicited by uncertainty regarding the historical value of the poem, which in turn is based primarily on two problems. These are: (1) the propriety of the Sihon clause in vs. 29d and (2) the apparent clash between the north-to-south movement of the poem and the south-to-north drive of the Israelites in the surrounding narrative. We observed above that the first problem insists on an outmoded poetic analysis and the second is only valid as long as we presume that poem and narrative describe the identical events. Once the poem is seen as a substantial witness of antiquity then vss. 26 and 31 become integral links between the poem and the accompanying narrative. Other objections are minor and can be accommodated satisfactorily within a concept which accepts this early tradition as having been handed down after the events it reports.

In sum, Miller's evaluation of the Heshbon tradition suffers from an uncritical acceptance of and *overreliance* on primarily literary-critical and traditio-historical analyses. It is to be regretted that in his article in *Israelite and Judean History* (1977a: 213-284), important works such as those by Van Zyl, Hanson, and Stuart, escaped his notice and he nowhere related his discussion of the written materials to recent research in comparative poetic analysis. While in his response to the Heshbon Symposium Miller's criticism of Hanson's circularity is appropriate (1977b: 3-4), Hanson's aim to find some external control from linguistic history which can be utilized in the discussion of both the Heshbon poem and narrative eludes him. We may also add that any correlation between the Heshbon tradition and Tell Hesban rests on the unproven assumption that biblical Heshbon and Tell Hesban are identical. Methodologically, it is out of order to draw too many inferences for the literary witness from Tell Hesban until the identity of these two locations has been established.

"The Israelite 'Conquest' and the Evidence from Transjordan," a contribution to the seventy-fifth anniversary of the founding of ASOR by M. Weippert (1979: 15-34), argues that the song fragments of Num 21:14-15 and vss. 27-31 [sic] are "unquestionably old, probably going back before the period of the monarchy" (17).[11] Upon further scrutiny Weippert confesses that he does not understand the *crux interpretum* (vs. 30), thinks that vs. 27 is not part of the song, and omits the Sihon clause in vs. 29d for metric reasons. Having emended the text of the poem, he concludes that it reports an Israelite military campaign against the

Moabites in which Israel did not take "the land between the territory of Heshbon and the Arnon, away from the Moabites" (21). Furthermore, the account describing the defeat of Sihon of Heshbon and the conquest of his kingdom by the Israelites is not an authentic historical tradition. Rather, "it is highly probable that this account is based on a fabrication or, to put it less harshly, that it was deduced from the designation of Heshbon as *qryt syhn*" (22).

Accepting his own interpretation of the poem, Weippert then registers a contradiction between the warlike clash between Israel and Moab in the poem and the peaceful coexistence between Israel and the surrounding nations presupposed in the narrative accounts (Num 21-22 and its later elaborations in Deut 2 and Judg 11). This contradiction "shows that the idea of a brotherly coexistence, in this early period, between Israel and its neighbors to the east is pure fiction" (23). What then is the function of the Sihon story in Num 21 and its later elaboration in Deut 2? The story serves "to bridge the geographical gap between the wilderness tradition and the Benjamite conquest tradition which had its starting-point in the *'rbwt mw'b*" (23).

In the remainder of the paper Weippert seeks to elucidate the settlement period in Transjordan following A. Alt's model of a peaceful settlement spreading from west to east and occasioning only intermittent clashes, like the one reflected in the song of Heshbon (32-34). Weippert suggests that the silence in extrabiblical Egyptian texts and the Amarna letters which had led to the conclusion that the area between Pella and Elath had no settled population is erroneous. He thinks the silence is not to be found in the history of the settlement but was politically motivated. This is apparent from archaeological excavations in the area which have established the presence of Middle and Late Bronze Age settlements (25-26).

Weippert, known for his extensive studies of Edom, has written a frank paper and developed a number of interesting suggestions. He must be commended for admitting to the immense textual difficulties of Num 21:30 and for his consequent refusal to stake too much of his reconstruction on this crux. His challenge to a number of erroneous conclusions regarding the settlement in Transjordan is daring and will have to be taken seriously alongside other recent evidence on the population in Central Moab (Miller 1979: 43-52; Kautz 1981: 27-35). Weippert is also correct in observing the generally peaceful relations between Israel and her neighbors in Transjordan though Num 22-24 testifies to some non-military friction between Israel and Moab. Unfortunately, he nowhere accounts for the fact that at least none of the Sihon conquest traditions reflects a peaceful process.

The contradiction he perceives between the alleged clash of Israelites and Moabites in the poem and the peaceful relations in the narratives depends entirely on his assumption that the poem reports a conflict between Israelites and Moabites. This in turn rests on

his emendations to the poem, which are unjustified in the light of recent studies in prosody and scansion noted above. Except in the interests of prior presuppositions, there are no insuperable reasons for the omission of the Sihon clause which anchors the poem to the Amorites. Such an emendation of a textually incontestable *lectio difficilior* is also discredited by the combined witness of biblical tradition. Hence the alleged contradiction between the poem and the narratives is entirely self-created. Similarly, the suggestion that the account of Sihon's defeat is based on a fabrication creates far more problems than it solves. Tension between Israel and Moab there was, but no open warlike conflict. Indeed it is the cumulative force of the problems created by Weippert's theory which calls its validity into question.

Summary and Conclusions

Our review of the critical literature during the last century has shown that the Sihon conquest tradition received somewhat passing scholarly notice until about 1968. Studies of the Heshbon stories converged primarily on Num 21:21-31 and only recently extended inquiry into the tradition recorded in Deut 2, Judg 11, and Jer 48:45-47. A variety of interpretations of the Heshbon tradition emerged and may be placed into three convenient groups.

Oldest and predominant is the view represented *mutatis mutandis* by critics such as Ewald, Dillmann, Heinisch, Rudolph, Noth, and R. de Vaux. All accept the priority of the Sihon account in Num 21 and interpret the story as an essentially historical description of the conflict between Israelites and Amorites from the early conquest and/or settlement period. Included in the account is a short reflection of an earlier clash between the Amorites and Moab. With the exception of R. de Vaux most critics attributed Num 21:21-31 to the Elohist source and traced certain redactional activity and deuteronomistic touches in the material. On this view the events narrated in Num 21:21-25 (and vs. 26), 31 are largely identified with those recounted in the poem, which is considered an Israelite taunt song (vss. 27-30).

This prevailing opinion has been seriously challenged since 1881 by E. Meyer and Stade. Meyer rejected the Sihon clause in vs. 29d because of its alleged metric irregularity and absence in Jer 48:45-47, and claimed that the opinion represented by Ewald did not account for the southward direction of events in the poem as against the northward movement of the surrounding prose narrative. Once deprived of elements which tied the poem to the conquest, Num 21:27-30 could be considered a triumphal ode which celebrated throughout the victory of Israel over Moab during the period of Omri. Meyer's skeptical attitude regarding the historical value of the poem was then extended to the prose narrative. His study did not lose its appeal, as is evident from more recent though divergent studies by Bartlett, Van Seters, and J. M. Miller.

While Bartlett agrees with Ewald as far as the priority and source of Num 21:21-25 is concerned, he contends for Meyer's interpretation of the poem even though he dates it to the time of David. Weippert, though acknowledging the antiquity of the poem, similarly accepts Meyer's objections to the conquest context of the poem. He suggests that the passage describing the defeat of Sihon of Heshbon was a fabrication rather than an authentic historical tradition.

Van Seters is the most consistent critic in developing Meyer's conclusions. He adopts Meyer's challenge against the Israelite-conquest interpretation of the poem and places it in the exilic context. He further insists that narrative and poem share the same fate. While the account in Num 21 is dependent upon Deuteronomy and Judges, the poem comes from a collection of taunt songs similar to those in the prophetic literature. Hence both narrative and poem belong to the exilic period and are not historically trustworthy. Indeed, the Sihon conquest narrative should be regarded as the result of a literary "artificial" development without any great antiquity.

While Miller's theory is uncritically selective, it holds to a Davidic date for the poem yet stresses that both poem and narrative give evidence of redactional activity and of a thoroughly deuteronomistic orientation.

A third category of interpretations also attributes the Heshbon account to the period of conquest and/or settlement without necessarily following Ewald's exposition of the tradition. Such accept the essential historicity of Num 21:21-31 for various reasons and include historians and critics (e.g., Bimson 1978, G. A. Smith, Glueck, Bright, Mendenhall, Aharoni, Ottosson, Van Zyl, Hanson, and Gilead).

Ottosson's rather unique study refuses the proposals of both Ewald and Meyer and attributes the Numbers account to a predeuteronomist P-traditionist. Retaining the Sihon clause, Ottosson suggests that the passage depicts Israel's defeat of Sihon and her future belligerence toward Moab as described in Num 22-24.

Van Zyl and Hanson see Num 21:27-30 as an Amorite victory song over Moab. Though Hanson's rather speculative endeavors to reconstruct the song in a hypothetical Amorite has not attracted many adherents, his basic suggestion that the song seems to conform to early Canaanite orthography is of considerable value. Van Zyl proposes that the accompanying narrative of Israel's defeat of Sihon the Amorite (Num 21:21-26) provides the appropriate setting for the poem sung by Amorites to commemorate their victory over Moab and reused by the invading Israelites to celebrate their success over the Amorites.

Another equally possible option would be to view the poem merely as a citation of an Amorite poem (sung earlier only by Amorites) incorporated in Num 21 as documentary evidence, and part of the author's extended explanation (recorded in vs. 26) that immediately prior to Israel's arrival Amorites had defeated the Moabites and deprived the latter of territory south toward the Arnon. It will probably never be clear whether Heshbon itself was ruined in this campaign or became simply the base of operations for the Moabite conquest. On this alternative vss. 26-30 would be an explanatory historical note parenthetical to the narrative of Num 21:21-31. Indeed, the account which breaks off at vs. 25 would continue without the slightest difficulty in vs. 31.

The interpretation that Num 21:21-31 describes Israel's victory over Sihon during the conquest period and utilizes an earlier poem celebrating an Amorite victory over Moab (transmitted in an early Israelite orthography) has much to commend itself:

1. It resolves the problem over the southward thrust of the poem setting Num 21:27-30 off from the northward direction of events in the prose narrative (Num 21:21-25). It also explains why the area in which the clash(es) traced in the poem is different from that described in the narrative. The location of Jahaz is nowhere alluded to in the song. Moreover, no antitheses between Israelite/Amorite and Amorite/Moabite clashes need be postulated for the poem, as it projects only an Amorite conquest of Moab.

2. Such a view of the poem also conforms to its larger context and requires no inherent alterations of the text. The words "therefore the ballad singers say" (vs. 27a) seem to suggest that the song once existed independently of its present context and relate the following song to vs. 26. In the light of recent studies in early Israelite orthography and Hebrew and Ugaritic poetry the more difficult but textually unquestioned reading "to an Amorite king, Sihon" embedded firmly in both song and narrative need not be emended in conformity with inflexible and antiquated methods of poetry scansion and meter. Retention of the Sihon clause also obviates somewhat awkward and unconvincing hypotheses which seek to account for this alleged gloss. The archaic orthography in the poem would further argue for its antiquity in the light of linguistic history.

3. Once the poem is accepted as ancient, the historical value of both poem and prose narrative need no longer be doubted. There is certainly no reason for discrediting the combined witness of biblical tradition that Sihon was an Amorite king. Similarly vs. 26 can be accepted as historically trustworthy. While there are later touches (e.g. vs. 25b), the basic unity of this passage can be safely assumed as can also the Sihon material in Deuteronomy and Judges.

4. The rather compact and theologically neutral story in Num 21:21-31 may be taken as an in-

dication of its priority over the Heshbon accounts in Deut 2 and Judg 11. In addition, both the similarities and differences between Num 21:27-30 and Jer 48:45-47 and the bits of older materials incorporated in Jer 48 are best explained by proposing Num 21:27-30's antiquity.

5. The above interpretation eliminates the need to conjecture elaborate reconstructions and misunderstandings of both poem and narrative alleged to have occurred so shortly after the event. It also obviates postulates of historical situations and functions of the tradition which have far less to commend them than the conquest context.

6. There is nothing incredible in the passage itself nor is anything gained by inventing the story at a later period. Theological and ideological concerns there are, but to reduce the passage to a mere artificial literary construct because of these assumes too much.

7. There are fewer difficulties raised by this theory than by those represented by Ewald and Meyer. Also it echoes indirectly the large group of scholars who prefer an early date for this episode.

Yet two questions remain. First, why would Israelite tradition reuse or incorporate an alien poem? Second, how is this analysis of the written OT sources to be related to the findings at Tell Hesban? The suggestion has been offered, and there is nothing unreasonable, inconsistent or impossible about it, that the Israelites (or at least the author of Num 21:21-31) utilized this short song to magnify their own victory over Sihon, who had only recently subjugated the Moabites, and thus sought to demonstrate their superiority and military prowess. In response to the second question, it should be remembered that the problem is largely created by the still unproven though widely accepted assumption that biblical Heshbon and Tell Hesban are identical. It should also be kept in mind that the written sources—so far only they tell us of Heshbon and Israel's conflict with Sihon the Amorite—provide the framework for interpreting the artifactual data, and not the reverse. This is not a cavalier response (or irresponsibility) to a problem; but rather it is methodologically imperative if we are to take seriously recent criticisms leveled against unjustified correlations between biblical and archaeological witnesses.

These problems are not insuperable and certainly are far outweighed by the gains of this interpretation. We have noted above that the various hypotheses regarding the Heshbon tradition provide plausible solutions; however, when considering the number of secondary explanations offered and that more evidence has to be explained away than can support these theories, it becomes apparent that little advantage is offered over the interpretation just considered. In sum, the theory that Num 21:21-31 and its later elaborations in Deuteronomy and Judges describe an Israelite victory over Sihon during the conquest period and incorporate an Amorite poem (Num 21:27-30) in early Hebrew orthography commemorating an earlier Amorite conquest of Moab, should be considered more seriously.

References

Abel, F. M.
1933   *Géographie de la Palestine*, vol. 1. Paris: Gabalda.

1938   Vol. 2.

Aharoni, Y.
1967   *The Land of the Bible*. Translated by A. F. Rainey. Philadelphia: Westminster.

Baentsch, B.
1903   *Exodus-Leviticus-Numeri*. HzAT. Göttingen: Vandenhoeck & Ruprecht.

Bartlett, J. R.
1969   The Historical Reference of Numbers XXl. 27-30. *Palestine Exploration Quarterly* 101: 94-100.

1970   Sihon and Og, Kings of the Amorites. *Vetus Testamentum* 20: 257-277.

1978   The Conquest of Sihon's Kingdom: A Literary Re-examination. *Journal of Biblical Literature* 97: 347-351.

Bimson, J. J.
1978   *Redating the Exodus and Conquest*. JSOT Suppl. Series 5. Sheffield: University of Sheffield.

Bright, J.
1965   *Jeremiah*. AB 21. Garden City: Doubleday.

1972   *A History of Israel*. 2d ed. OTL. London: SCM Press.

Buchanan, G. W.
1974   Has the Griesbach Hypothesis Been Falsified? *Journal of Biblical Literature* 93: 550-572.

Coats, G. W.
1976   Conquest Traditions in the Wilderness Theme. *Journal of Biblical Literature* 95: 177-190.

Cross, F. M., and Freedman, D. N.
1952   *Early Hebrew Orthography: A Study of the Epigraphic Evidence*. AOS 36. New Haven, CT: American Oriental Society.

1975   *Studies in Ancient Yahwistic Poetry*. SBLDS 21. Missoula: Scholars Press.

Dillmann, A.
1886 *Numeri, Deuteronomium und Josua*. 2d ed. Leipzig: Hirzel.

Ewald, H.
1883 *The History of Israel*. 4th ed. Vol 2. London: Longmans.

Farmer, W. R.
1964 *The Synoptic Problem*. New York: Macmillan.

Fritz, V.
1970 *Israel in der Wüste*. MTS 7. Marburg: N. G. Elwert.

Gilead, H.
1977 The Song of the Mōšĕlîm (Num 21:27-30). *Beth Mikra* 23: 12-17 (Hebrew).

Glueck, N.
1940 *The Other Side of the Jordan*. New Haven, CT. American Schools of Oriental Research.

Gray, G. B.
1903 *Numbers*. ICC. Edinburgh: T. & T. Clark.

Gunn, D. M.
1974 The "Battle Report": Oral or Scribal Convention? *Journal of Biblical Literature* 93: 513-518.

Hanson, P. D.
1968 The Song of Heshbon and David's NÎR. *Harvard Theological Review* 61: 291-320.

Heinisch, P.
1936 *Das Buch Numeri*. Bonn: Hanstein.

Holzinger, H.
1903 *Numeri*. Tübingen: J. C. B. Mohr (P. Siebeck).

Kautz, J. R.
1981 Tracking the Ancient Moabites. *Biblical Archaeologist* 44: 27-35.

Mendenhall, G. E.
1962 The Hebrew Conquest of Palestine. *Biblical Archaeologist* 25: 66-87.

Meyer, E.
1881 Kritik der Berichte über die Eroberung Palaestinas. *Zeitschrift für die alttestamentliche Wissenschaft* 1: 117-146.

1885 Der Krieg gegen Sîchon und die zugehörigen Abschnitte. *Zeitschrift für die alttestamentliche Wissenschaft* 5: 36-52.

Miller, J. M.
1977a The Israelite Occupation of Canaan. Pp. 213-284 in *Israelite and Judean History*, eds. J. H. Hayes and J. M. Miller. OTL. Philadelphia: Westminster.

1977b Response to L. Geraty's 'Heshbon in the Bible, Literary Sources, and Archaeology.' Presented at the *Heshbon Symposium* Dec. 29, 1977 in San Francisco, CA.

1979 Archaeological Survey of Central Moab. 1978. *Bulletin of the American Schools of Oriental Research* 234: 43-52.

Mittmann, S.
1973 Num 21, 14-21—eine redaktionelle Komposition. Pp. 143-49 in *Wort und Geschichte: Festschrift für K. Elliger zum 70. Geburtstag*, eds. H. Gese and H. P. Rüger. AOAT 18. Kevelaer: Butzon & Bercker.

1975 *Deuteronomium 1, 1-6, 3 literarkritisch und traditionsgeschichtlich untersucht*. BZAW 139. Berlin: de Gruyter.

Moriarty, F. L.
1968 *Numbers*. The Jerome Biblical Commentary. Englewood Cliffs, NJ: Prentice-Hall.

Mowinckel, S.
1964 *Tetrateuch-Pentateuch-Hexateuch*. Berlin: Töpelmann.

Noth, M.
1940 Num 21 als Glied der "Hexateuch"-Erzählung. *Zeitschrift für die alttestamentliche Wissenschaft* 58: 161-189.

1944 Israelitische Stämme zwischen Ammon und Moab. *Zeitschrift für die alttestamentliche Wissenschaft* 60: 11-57.

1968 *Numbers*. Translated by J. D. Martin. OTL. London: SCM Press.

1972 *A History of Pentateuchal Traditions*. Translated and introduced by B. W. Anderson. Englewood Cliffs, NJ: Prentice-Hall.

Orchard, B.
1976 *Matthew, Luke and Mark*. Manchester: Koinonia.

Ottosson, M.
1969 *Gilead, Tradition and History*. Lund: Gleerup.

Rendtorff, R.
1977 *Das überlieferungsgeschichtliche Problem des Pentateuch*. BZAW 147. Berlin: de Gruyter.

Richter, W.
1966 *Traditionsgeschichtliche Untersuchungen zum Richterbuch*. Bonn: Hanstein.

Rudolph, W.
1938 *Der "Elohist" von Exodus bis Josua*. BZAW 68. Berlin: A. Töpelmann.

Schmid, H. H.
1976 *Der sogenannte Jahwist: Beobachtungen und Fragen zur Pentateuchforschung*. Zürich: Theologischer Verlag.

Shea, W. H.
1979 Heshbon in Iron Age History. *American Schools of Oriental Research Symposium*. November 15, 1979.

Simons, J.
1947 Two Connected Problems Relating to the Israelite Settlement in Trans-Jordan. *Palestine Exploration Quarterly* 79: 27-39; 87-101.

Smith, G. A.
n.d. *The Historical Geography of the Holy Land*. 22ed. London: Hodder & Stoughton.

Snaith, N. H.
1969 *Leviticus and Numbers*. NCB. London: Oliphants.

Stade, B.
1881 Nachwort des Herausgebers. *Zeitschrift für die alttestamentliche Wissenschaft* 1: 146-147.

Streeter, B. H.
1925 *The Four Gospels: A Study of Origins*. London: Macmillan.

Stuart, D. K.
1976 *Studies in Early Hebrew Meter*. HSM 13. Missoula: Scholars Press.

Sturdy, J.
1976 *Numbers*. Cambridge Bible Commentary. Cambridge: Cambridge University Press.

Sumner, W. A.
1968 Israel's Encounters with Edom, Moab, Ammon, Sihon, and Og According to the Deuteronomist. *Vetus Testamentum* 18: 216-228.

Talbert, C. H., and McKnight, E. V.
1972 Can the Griesbach Hypothesis Be Falsified? *Journal of Biblical Literature* 91: 338-368.

Van Seters, J.
1972 The Conquest of Sihon's Kingdom: A Literary Examination. *Journal of Biblical Literature* 91: 182-197.

1975 *Abraham in History and Tradition*. New Haven, CT: Yale University.

1976 Oral Patterns or Literary Conventions in Biblical Narrative. *Semeia* 5: 139-154.

1980 Once Again—The Conquest of Sihon's Kingdom. *Journal of Biblical Literature* 99: 117-119.

Van Zyl, A. H.
1960 *The Moabites*. POS 3. Leiden: E. J. Brill.

Vaulx, J. de
1972 *Les Nombres*. Sources bibliques. Paris: Gabalda.

Vaux, R. de
1941 Notes d'histoire et de topographie Transjordaniennes. *Vivre et Penser* 1: 16-25.

1978 *The Early History of Israel*. Translated by D. Smith. London: Darton, Longman & Todd.

Weippert, M.
1979 The Israelite "Conquest" and the Evidence from Transjordan. In *Symposia Celebrating the Seventy-fifth Anniversary of the Founding of the American Schools of Oriental Research (1900-1975)*, ed. F. M. Cross. Cambridge, MA: American Schools of Oriental Research.

Wüst, M.
1975 *Untersuchungen zu den siedlungsgeographischen Texten des Alten Testaments, I. Ostjordanland*. Wiesbaden: Reichert.

Endnotes

[1]Heinisch and Rudolph essentially espoused the position of Ewald.

[2]Similarly Noth and later Bartlett (1970: 257-277) argued for narrower geographical confines for Sihon's and Israel's territory. J. Simons (1947: 27-39, 87-101) challenged this reconstruction and explanation of the phrase "from Arnon to the Jabbok." Simons claimed that the biblical evidence suggests that the region between these two rivers once belonged to the Ammonites "before it passed into the hands of the Amorites, and continued to be called after them" (90). Simons distinguished three successive periods in the political history of Middle Transjordan during which the territory was a political unity, first administered by Ammonites, then Amorites, and finally by Israelites (90; *cf.* Abel 1933: 277). He claims
> gebûl benê 'ammon is neither the frontier of the Ammonites at any period, nor the territory of the Ammonites at the time of Moses and Sihon, but their former territory from 'Arnon to Yabboq' which was still designated as 'the land of the Bene Ammon'

and as such was claimed back from Jephthah by the king of Ammon (96). Though de Vaux rejected Simons' study as of little value (1978: 565 n. 39) Simons has demonstrated some weaknesses in de Vaux's assessment of the extent of Sihon's kingdom (Simons 1947: 91-93). Nevertheless, while some of Simons' arguments appear forced and the Ammonites may have never occupied the *whole* area between the Arnon and the Jabbok, the suggestion of a possible Ammonite prehistory for at least parts of this region is worthy of further investigation particularly in the light of the claims recorded in Josh 13:25 and Judg 11:13.

³Noth argued:

Die vor allem bei der literarischen Analyse der Genesis bewährten Resultate der Quellenscheidung, die in der Regel zu der mehr oder weniger lückenlosen Zusammenstellung der ursprünglichen Quellen geführt hat, haben sich bei den verschiedenen Vorschlägen einer Aufteilung von Num 21:21-31 in keiner Weise ergeben. Aus methodischen Gründen muss Einspruch erhoben werden gegen die Begründung einer Quellenscheidung auf vereinzelte und unter sich weder formal noch sachlich zusammenhängende Unebenheiten im Text; die Erfahrung lehrt, dass dadurch die Quellenscheidung zu einer Schraube ohne Ende wird und sich zu Unrecht selbst ad absurdum führt . . . (1940: 164).

Much of the difficulty surrounding Num 21:24-25 is based on the idea that the demonstrative pronoun *'elleh* must refer back to what has gone before. This has contributed to the assumption that there must have been a list of cities which has dropped out. However, neither Baentsch nor later commentators take into account the use of *'elleh* to designate an item which follows (*e.g.* Gen 2:4; 6:9; 11:10; 39:19; Num 16:28). *Cf.* Ottosson (1969: 56-57), who rejects Noth's evaluation of vss. 24-25.

⁴Among writers who had attributed all or part of Num 21:21-31 to the Elohist source are Smith (n.d.: 663), Gray (1903: 294); Holzinger (1903: 98-100); Baentsch (1903: 581); Rudolph (1938: 39-40).

⁵However, de Vaux remained unconvinced because the word "Amorites" instead of "Canaanites" has "little meaning beyond the Jordan, which defined the boundary of Canaan" (1978: 565; similarly Van Seters 1972: 182).

⁶This is denied by Ottosson who writes "presumably this is the reverse of the truth" (1969: 56; *cf.* the objection of Van Zyl [1960: 113]).

⁷Note the serious questions being raised about the present status of Pentateuchal studies and the assumptions of Gunkel, von Rad, Noth, and Koch that the disciplines of literary criticism and tradition criticism complement each other, as well as the problems involved in the attempt to trace the development of the smallest units of tradition to the final literary stages (*e.g.* Van Seters 1975; Schmid 1976; Rendtorff 1977).

⁸Similarly, Y. Aharoni in his historical geography of the Holy Land states that the Heshbon tradition is ancient, trustworthy, and has its historical background in the conquest period (1967: 187-188).

⁹As listed in Streeter (1926: 151-152). However, the question of synoptic relations is currently being re-evaluated in the works of Farmer (1964), Talbert and McKnight (1972: 338-368), Buchanan (1974: 550-572), and Orchard (1976).

¹⁰Van Seters' more recent and justified criticism (1980: 119) of the literary reconstructions of these texts by S. Mittmann (1973: 143-149, 1975: 79-93) and M. Wüst (1975) demonstrates the unfortunate but real disagreements which divide literary critics. One is reminded of S. Mowinckel's ferocious yet not wholly unfounded criticism of Noth's analysis of Num 32 in which he accused the latter of dissolving the chapter into an immense series of interpolations with interpolations squeezed into the interpolations and glosses added to the secondary interpolations and all of this in the process of a minute hair-splitting literary-critical method (1964: 55). Mittmann's literary-critical examination in particular appears to be such an occidental Procrustean bed which not only leads to a *reductio ad absurdum* but also is insensitive to the dynamics of literary process and change.

While no critic can afford to ignore responsible literary analysis, restraint must be exercised against invoking so many redactors and glossators as to leave OT criticism open to charges of circular reasoning and extreme subjectivity. Since, however, the priority of the Numbers account does not depend on the excessively complex theory of traditio-historical and redactional relationships advanced by Mittmann and Wüst, our criticism of their source analyses in no way invalidates the possible antiquity of the Sihon tradition. Aside from Mittmann and Wüst (1975: 18 n. 54), V. Fritz (1970: 28) had argued for the priority of Num 21:21-31. It is to be regretted that the work by Wüst never took account of the studies by Sumner (1968: 216-228), Hanson (1968: 297-320) and Van Seters (1972: 182-197).

¹¹Vaulx comments: "Ce chant est ancien, sa langue archaïque . . . il pourrait bien être contemporain des evenements . . ." (1972: 245).

Appendix A

HESHBON THROUGH THE CENTURIES

Werner K. Vhymeister

Appendix A

Heshbon Through the Centuries

Date	In Territory of	Under the Empire of	Date—Specific References to the City
15th B.C.	Moab	_____	15th B.C. (Num 21:30)
15th B.C. 2nd half	Amorites (Sihon)	_____	15th B.C., 2nd half (Num 21:26-32)
14th B.C.	Israelites	_____	14th B.C. (Num 21:25, 34; Deut 1:4; Josh 13:26; etc.) Early 14th B.C. (Num 32:37; Josh 21:1, 39; cf. 1 Chr 6:81)
ca. 1316 - *ca.*1298	Moab (Eglon)	_____	_____
ca. 1298 - *ca.*1106	Israelites	_____	1406/05-*ca.* 1106/05 (Judg 11:26)
ca. 1106 - *ca.*1100	Ammon-Moab	_____	_____
ca. 1100 - 931	Israelites	_____	Between 971-931 (Cant 7:4)
931 - *ca.* 800	Israel[1]	_____	_____
ca. 800 - *ca.* 760	Moab (?)	_____	_____
ca. 760 - *ca.* 734	Judah (?)	_____	_____
ca. 734 - *ca.* 733	Moab (Salamanu)	_____	_____
ca. 733 - 605	Moab[2]	Assyria	*ca.* 700 (Isa 15:4; 16:8, 9)
605 - *ca.* 595	Moab	Babylon	Between 605/04-*ca.* 595 (Jer 48:2, 34, 45)
ca. 595 - 582	Ammon	Babylon (?)	*ca.* 595-*ca.* 594/93 (Jer 49:3)
582 - ?	Bedouins	Babylon[3]	_____
5th B.C. - 4th B.C.	Tobiads (?)	Persia	_____
3rd B.C. - 198	Moabitis (?)	Ptolemies	_____
198 - *ca.* 164	Moabitis	Seleucids	2nd B.C. (*Ant.* 12.4.11)
ca. 164 - 63	Maccabeans[4]	_____	Between 103-76/75 (*Ant.* 12.15.4)
63 - 37	Nabateans (?)	Rome	_____
37 - 4	Herod	Rome	Between 37-4 B.C. (*Ant.* 15.8.5)

Date	In Territory of	Under the Empire of	Dates—Specific References to the City
ca 4 B.C.-A.D. 105	Nabateans[5]	Rome	1st A.D. (*Wars* 3.3.3; Pliny, *Nat. Hist.* 5.12[?]) A.D. 66 (*Wars* 2.18.1)
106 - 330	*Provincia Arabia*	Rome	Between A.D. 130-160 (Ptolemy *Geog* 5.17) 218-222 (coins of Elagabalus) 219, 236, 288 (milestones 5, 6, road Esbus-Livias) 325 (Council of Nicaea)
330 - 635	*Provincia Arabia*	Byzantines	Before 340 (Eusebius, *Onom* 84:1-6; etc.) 364-375 (milestones 5, road Esbus-Livias) *ca.* 400 (Egeria) 431 (Council of Ephesus) 451 (Council of Chalcedon) *ca.* 570 (*Notitia Antiochena*) *ca.* 590 (capital in church, *Râs es-Siâghah*) *ca.* 605 (Georges of Cyprus) *ca.* 600 (mosaic of Ma'in)
635 - 750	Jund of Damascus; later Palestine	Caliphate: Orthodox, then Umayyad after 661	649 (letters of Pope Martin I)
750 - 877	Province of Syria	Abbasid Caliphate	Al-Tabari (839-923)
877 - 904	_____	Tulunids	_____
904 - 941	_____	Abbasids	_____
941 - 969	_____	Ikhshids	_____
969 - 1070s	_____	Fatimids	_____
1070s - 1100s	_____	Seljuqs	_____
1100s- 1187/8	disputed area	Crusaders/ Muslim conflict	_____
1187/8- 1250	probably the province of Damascus	Ayyubids	12th century (Behâ ed-Dîn)
1250 - 1516/7	Damascus; occasionally al-Kerak	Mamluks, then Bedouins	14th century, numerous Arab authors; ha-Parchi
1516/7 -1831	Damascus	Ottoman Empire (titular; often simply Bedouin)	_____

Date	In Territory of	Under the Empire of	Dates—Specific References to the City
1831 - 1840	Syria	Egypt - Muhammad 'Ali	Western travellers' accounts
1840 - 1918	Damascus	Ottoman Empire	Western travellers' accounts
1918 - 1920	Occupied Enemy Territory: East	Damascus Arab government	_____
1920 - 1921	Local Ad- ministrators	(British influence)	_____
1921 - 1946	al-Belqa	Emirate of Trans- Jordan	Western travellers' accounts
1946 - present	al-Belqa	Kingdom of Jordan	Western travellers' accounts

Endnotes

[1]Hazael of Damascus invaded the land during the reign of Jehu of Israel (841-814).

[2]Moab rebelled against Assyria (ca. 713-711), and a century later ceased to be subject to Assyria (before 605 B.C.) since Nineveh was destroyed in 612 B.C.

[3]Until 539 B.C.

[4]In theory the Maccabeans were under the Seleucids until 104 B.C.

[5]At the beginning of the Jewish War (A.D. 66), Esbus was sacked by the Jews. The Nabatean hold on the territory was most likely not uninterrupted during this period.

Appendix B

HESBAN IN THE LITERARY
SOURCES SINCE 1806

Werner K. Vhymeister

Hesban in the Literary Sources Since 1806

Beginning with U. J. Seetzen (1806), and ending with Bernhard W. Anderson (1964) just a few years before the first archaeological campaign on Tell Hesban took place in 1968, descriptions of the ruins of Hesban and its vicinity as seen by—mainly—Western visitors, are given in this Appendix B.

The first known Western visitor to Hesban in the 19th century was the German traveler Seetzen. Arriving Sunday, March 22, 1806, he wrote in his diary:

... Half an hour later we came to Hüsban, located on a high hill which consists almost exclusively of naked limestone. Except for some overturned pillars nothing of importance is found here. On the left side of the road there was a pool cased with stones besides [sic] which we met some cattle and some Arabian herdsmen. Westward, not far from Hüsban, the Nahr Hüsban springs forth, which flows into the Jordan. Along this little river some mills should be located ... (1854: 406-407).

John S. Buckingham visited Hesban in 1816 (Tobler 1867: 143). Of his *Travels* is the following quotation:

The large reservoir to the south of the town, and about half a mile from the foot of the hill on which it stands, is constructed with good masonry, and not unlike the cisterns of Solomon, near Jerusalem, to which it is also nearly equal in size.[1]

In 1816-1817 Charles Leonard Irby and James Mangles also visited the Near East (Tobler 1867: 145). Of their visit to Hesban they wrote: "The ruins are uninteresting, and the only pool we saw was too insignificant to be one of those mentioned in Scripture." In two of the cisterns among the ruins they found about three dozen human skulls and bones. They regarded them as an illustration of Gen 37:20.[2]

Edward Robinson, of New York, who visited Palestine in 1838 (Tobler 1867: 162), mentions that he looked up to Wadi Hesban from the Ghor, and adds that near it, "far up in the mountain is the ruined place of the same name, the ancient Heshbon." Then Robinson explains that "neither of these places was visible from Jericho" (1841: 278-279).

J. L. Porter, who visited Palestine in 1854 and 1857 (Tobler 1867: 189),[3] also visited Hesban. He mentions that towards the western part of the hill there is a singular structure, whose crumbling ruins exhibit the workmanship of successive ages—the massive stones of the Jewish period, the sculptured cornice of the Roman era, and the light Saracenic arch, all grouped together.[4]

... a green knoll, with rugged heaps of stones, rising above the surrounding plateau, and a little retired from its brow. ...

Moab is here a vast table land, on the brow of which, to the west, the crest is a little elevated, and to the eastward of it a slight depression of three or four miles in extent, beyond which the rounded hills rise 200 feet, and gently slope away to the east. In the centre of this depression is a small hill, of perhaps 200 feet high, but entirely isolated, with a little stream running past it on the east. This is Heshbon. The hill is one heap of shapeless ruin, while all the neighbouring slopes are full of caves, which have once been occupied, turned into use as habitations. The citadel hill has also a shoulder and a spur to the south, likewise covered with ruins. The summit of the hill is flattened; and here is a level platform, with Doric columns broken from their pedestals, and the foundations of a forum, or public building of the Roman period, arranged exactly like the Forum at Pompeii. The whole city must have had the circuit of about a mile. Some portions of the walls are standing—a few tiers of worn stones, and the space is thickly strewn with piles of Doric shafts, capitals of columns, broken entablatures, and large stones with the broad bevelled edge. In one edifice, of which a large portion remains, near the foot of the hill, Jewish stones, Roman arches, Doric pillars, and Saracenic arches, are all strangely mingled.

Below the city, to the east, are the remains of watercourses, and an enormous cistern, or fishpond, doubtless alluded to in Canticles ... (vii.4); and the old wells are so numerous, that we had to ride with great care to avoid them.

November 12-13, 1863, de Saulcy visited Hesban with "Capitaine d'Etat-Major Gelis" who made a plan of the ruins (fig. B.1). De Saulcy's description (1865: 279-282) is as follows:

When we arrived in Hesban, our disappointment was great; we had expected to find ruins comparable to those of 'Ammân, and we did not have under our eyes but masses of shapeless debris that, undoubtedly, came from rather recent times.

Fig. B.1   Plan of the ruins of Hesban (after de Saulcy 1865)

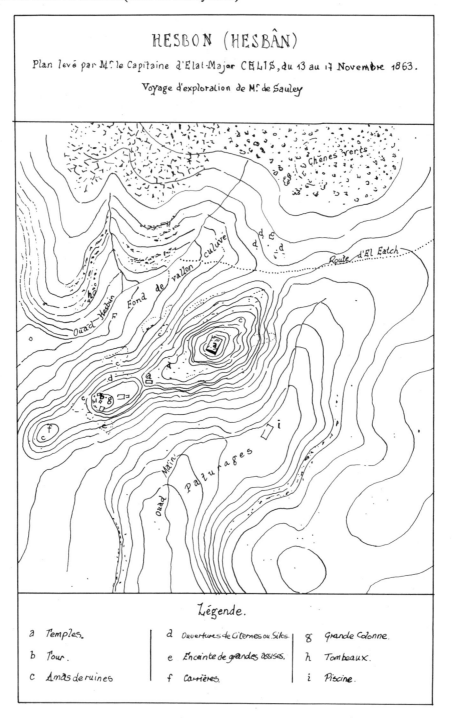

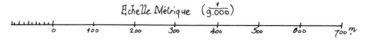

Two great hillocks, stretching from the southwest to the northeast, served as seat of the ancient city. The valley proper of Wâdī Hesbân opens to the north of these two plateaus. . . . To the south, the same hillocks give birth to the Wâdī Ma'în, at the bottom of which there is a pool of very great size. . . .

. . . The northern plateau is completely covered by masses of shapeless ruins, in whose midst there are numerous pools. In the center of this plateau there is a rectangular enclosure that seems to have surrounded a temple. This enclosure, made of big rows of masonry, about forty meters long and thirty wide, is oriented almost north to south, as the one of 'Arâq-el-Emîr. On the south end there is a base of an aedicule[5] of small dimension (about fifteen by eight meters). This one is oriented from east to west. This plateau is about two hundred and fifty meters long by a hundred wide; and it is completely covered, as the beginning of the slopes also, by heaps of debris. The second plateau, the one on the southwest, is as long, but only half as wide as the first one. It is also covered by ruins, but in the part that is closer to the north. There is still found the location of a temple, twenty meters long by fifteen wide, also oriented from east to west. About fifty meters to the west of this temple the remains of a square tower are visible, and between these two monuments there is a great column lying on the ground; it is of rough workmanship. The southern end of this second plateau shows quarries preceded by piles of debris. These are separated from the rest of the ruins by an empty interval of about two hundred meters.

To sum up, the ruins of Hesbân are just what we thought of them at first glance, that is, of very little interest. The enclosure made of big courses of masonry, of which I have talked before, is undoubtedly of Arabic construction, judging by the material used in it. About the temple that is surrounded, its location is marked only by the bases of some columns that remained in place, and these bases, being Roman, seem to be of a very low period. . . .

De Saulcy mentions that he asked some Arabs who had gathered around the visitors if they had found coins [*médailles*] on the ground. They answered that they had found them often, but after looking at them, they always threw them back (1865: 280).

Another interesting item, mentioned by de Saulcy (1865: 280), is the remains found around the bottom of the wadi that begins on the northern side of the tell, where they pitched their tents:

Around our camp, at the bottom of the wâdī, as also on the two flanks, the ground is sowed with great cubes of mosaic; with them found some small fragments of old glazed vessels. . . .

Their camp was established against a rocky flank of the wadi that had some tombs cut in the rock (de Saulcy 1865: 279-280). All of these tombs, says de Saulcy

have served or serve at present as lodging to the Bedouins that have brought their flocks to Hesbân. One of these tombs is much better preserved than the others. It still has its stone door, with hinges in the mass [of the rock], that is three fourths buried. The room to which one enters has niches for coffins on its lateral walls, and on the rear wall a little square chamber opens, flanked by two niches for coffins. All in this opening is terribly covered with dirt, and it is evident that, probably for centuries, it has served as a retreat to the Arab shepherds (1865: 287-288).

Among the items not mentioned by de Saulcy is any human settlement in or around Hesban. He mentions only Arab shepherds. No sign of a village is suggested in the plan made by Captain Gelis. There is no clear mention of a village, either, in the reports of the previous visitors of the 19th century.[6]

De Saulcy has included in his book a topographical chart, entitled "Reconnaissance de l'Ammonitide," made also by Captain Gelis, in 1863. In this chart the road from Amman to the south takes a sharp turn to the west-northwest just before reaching Hesban, and then passes between the tell and the wadi that starts just north of the ruins, in a southwestern direction.

Conder visited Hesban in 1881. In his report on his visit he has this much to say (1882: 8):

Shapeless mounds of hewn stones, rude pillars and cornices of Byzantine origin, a great pool on the east, a ruined fort on the south, numerous caves and cisterns with remains of a colonnaded building on the highest part of the hill, are all that we found.

In one of his books (1892: 142) Conder comments: "The ruins at Hesban, on the edge of the plateau high above the spring, are those of a large Roman town, but present nothing of special interest." Then, focusing on a particular item, he adds:

. . . The steep path from the valley leads through a sort of cutting which may once have been closed by a gate. This cutting stands out conspicuous on the skyline as seen from the stream, and recalls the words, 'Thine eyes—pools in Heshbon, by the gate of Bath Rabbim' (Cant. vii.4). 'The gate of the daughter of great ones' might perhaps have here led to the fishpools, which occur all along the stream.

Two significant elements in this comment are: suggested identifications of (a) "the gate of Bath-rabbim" and (b) "the fishpools in Heshbon" of Cant 7:4.

About the "gate" Conder gives more detail in his (1882: 8) report. After mentioning the "bright pools in the stream which runs beneath Heshbon on the west," he adds:

. . . The plateau on the edge of which the city stands is reached, from this stream, by an ancient road which, at the top of the ascent, passes through a sort of passage cut in the rocks about 8 or 10 feet high and 3 or 4 yards wide. This entry to the site of Heshbon from the north-west is known as the *Bueib* or 'gates,' and these gates looking down on the fishpools of Heshbon may perhaps be those noticed by the author of the Song of Songs under the name Bath Rabbim "Daughter of great ones."

Heidet writes that if a city-gate is meant, it must have been on the northern side of the southwestern hillock, because the main road of the region has always run at the foot of that hillock.[7] But he also points out that the name *Bath-Rabbim* is applied by the LXX and the Vulgate to the city and not to the gate (1903: cols. 659-660).[8]

Simons states that *Bath-Rabbim* "might be taken as a place name." But, if so, "the correct reading would be 'BETH-RABBIM'" since there are no examples of topographical *bath*-names. The context—he continues—suggests a major locality, presumably to be looked for in Transjordan. If this is so, then it would "almost certainly have alluded to RABBAH of the Ammonites." But, Simons concludes, "the text does not exclude . . . the possibility that a gate of HESHBON itself was called 'sha'ar bath-rabbīm', whatever the meaning or origin of such a name may be" (1959: 536).

About "the fishpools in Heshbon," Thomson writes:

When encamped here with Dr. Merrill, I rode for some distance along the banks below the fountain to see the little pools made by the stream, in which there were many small fishes. As we have already observed, it has been supposed that the royal poet referred to them in his 'Song,' when he compares the eyes of the 'prince's daughter' to 'the fishpools of Heshbon.' There never was either fountain of running stream in that city on the elevated plateau above 'Ain [sic] Hesbân nor sparkling pools; only dark cisterns or open tanks of rain-water in which fish cannot live (1885: 667).

But Thomson also suggests that the pools could have been similar to the ruined reservoir—about 30 m long by 20 m wide according to Heidet (1903: col. 660)—whose ruins can be seen to the southeast of the tell (1885: 661).

George E. Post, who visited Hesban on April 28, 1886, wrote:

The present ruins are not of high antiquity, and it is a difficult task for the imagination to restore to the reservoir to the east of the castle the beauty which made the fishpool of Heshbon a suitable simile for the eyes of Solomon's bride (1888: 190).

It has been already seen that Tristram (1865: 540) considered that the "fishpond" was the great pool alluded to also by Thomson.

Heidet (1903: col. 660) thinks that the "pools" are the large and numerous cisterns found at the southwest end of the hill. He remarks that many are uncovered today (that is, they have no roof) either because they were built that way, or because the vaulted roof collapsed. He points to them because they are close to the city gate (*cf.* Cant 7:4).

Thomson's description of the ruins of Hesban (1885: 661) adds a few details to the ones already found in other descriptions. He writes:

The ruins at Hesbân cover the sides and summit of an elongated double tell, less than two hundred feet high. Many of the houses and other edifices were evidently built by the Romans, and they were originally more substantial than those of other cities in this region, but none of them are of any special interest. The existing remains are mostly those of prostrate habitations, amongst which are columns, capitals, entablatures, old walls, and massive foundations. Upon the highest part of the tell is a fine pavement in good preservation, which may have belonged to a temple; and on the southwest side of the mound are the walls, almost entire, of a large, singular edifice with some broken columns about it, and exhibiting specimens of Jewish, Roman, and Saracenic architecture. But more than most ancient sites, Hesbân abounds in large vaulted chambers and bottle-shaped cisterns, some of them hewn in the rock, and which may date back to remote antiquity. The city must have depended upon cisterns for its supply of water, for the nearest permanent fountain is at 'Ain Hesbân in the deep valley below it, and distant more than half an hour to the northwest—a most inconvenient resource for the inhabitants of the ancient town at all times, and entirely unsafe in time of war.

Paul-M. Sejourné, reporting on his visit to Hesban on April 21, 1892, writes (1893: 136-137):

The ruins of Heshbon . . . are very difficult to determine period by period. Nevertheless we can clearly distinguish the high city and the low city. In the first one we can recognize the fortress, the surrounding walls and a monument with columns that I believe to be a temple; the second one is entirely buried; we can only see one of the pools in the eastern valley to the south.

Although he himself apparently was not a visitor to Hesban, Heidet adds a few details that are not found in the descriptions already presented. Writing about the "rectangular enclosure" of de Saulcy's "northern plateau" he adds (1903: col. 659) that

the interior is still partially paved with great and thick paving stones from which rise three or four column bases of cubical shape. The monument is approached by a great stairway located on the northern side, where some steps partially covered by dirt can be seen. Was this building a castle-fortress, a palace, a temple? . . . the column bases seem to belong to the Greco-Roman Period and the enclosing wall looks more like the work of the Arabs.

Alois Musil, who visited Hesban at the beginning of this century, mentions as part of the ruins a church with internal apse (Saller and Bagatti 1949: 226).[9]

Garstang (1931: 384) refers to the tell as follows:

This is a large mound . . . partly under cultivation, so that without excavation it is not possible to determine the outline of the city, nor to affirm that it was walled. None the less, the traces of occupation in M.B.A. and L.B.A. are plentiful all over its slopes, and the superficial potsherds bear a marked resemblance to the local types of Jericho, which is just visible from its summit. . . . In the vicinity are other, smaller Bronze Age sites, doubtless its dependencies.

Glueck also visited Hesban, as part of his surface survey of Eastern Palestine. He writes (1934: 6):

The top of the hill is covered primarily with Roman ruins, over and next to which some later Arabic ruins are visible. Although the site was carefully examined for pottery remains indicative of the early history of Heshbon, only one sherd was found belonging to E[arly] I[ron] I. A few nondescript sherds were picked up which may have been Nabatean and Roman, and a number of pieces of sigillata ware were found. There were large quantities of mediaeval Arabic glazed and painted sherds. We remained only long enough to scour the slopes and tops of the hills for sherds.[10]

Thirty years after Glueck's visit, Bernhard W. Anderson, annual professor of the American Schools of Oriental Research, in Jerusalem, also visited Hesban. He reports (1964: 1-2):

. . . At Hesban, which is only a short distance south of William Reed's sounding at Tell el-'Al, we were in for a big surprise. Nelson Glueck reported finding only one Iron Age sherd on the tell, but our surface finds, analyzed by the School's Director Paul Lapp, disclosed no less that nine items from Iron I, including a figurine head. . . .

Based on the previous reports, the following composite description of the ruins of Hesban, before excavations began in 1968, can be made.

The ruins of Hesban are located mainly on two hills about 60 m high above the plain. The hills stretch from the northeast to the southwest for about 550 m and are flanked by wadis on the northwest and the southeast. The perimeter of the old city was about 1.6 km.

The tell is partly under cultivation, so it is not possible, without excavations, to determine the outline of the city. Some portions of the walls are standing.

On the tell, the space is thickly strewn with piles of Doric shafts, capitals, broken entablatures, old walls, massive foundations, and debris. Among these ruins, several structures can be distinguished.

The northeastern hill is about 250 m long and 100 m wide. Its summit is flat. In the center there is a rectangular enclosure, 40 m long by 30 m wide, oriented almost from north to south. It is made of large rows of masonry, apparently of Arabic construction. The remains of what could have been a temple are inside the enclosure. Part of a fine pavement in good state of preservation, made of great and thick stones, is still visible there. Three or four column bases of cubical shape rise from the pavement. They belong to the Greco-Roman period. Broken Doric pillars lie on the ground. This monument is approached by a great stairway located on the northern side, where some steps, partially covered by dirt, can be seen.

On the southwestern end of this hill, near its foot, lies the base of a building, 15 m long by 8 m wide, oriented from east to west. The walls are "almost entire." The building exhibits massive stones of the Jewish period, Roman arches and Roman sculptured cornices, Doric pillars, and Saracenic arches, all strangely mixed.

The rest of the northeastern hill is covered by heaps of debris. It also has numerous bottle-shaped cisterns and vaulted chambers, especially on the southwestern side. Many of the cisterns are uncovered today. Perhaps their roofs collapsed, or they were made without roofs.

The southwestern hill is about 250 m long by 50 m wide. It is about 8 m lower than the other hill. It also has several cisterns. The ruined structures are located here mainly in its northeastern section. At the center of its flattened summit are the remains of a temple, 20 m long by 15 m wide, oriented from east to west. About 50 m to the west of the temple, the remains of a square tower are visible. Between these two monuments a great column of rough workmanship lies on the ground. On the southwestern end are some quarries, preceded by piles of debris (which also abound in the northeastern, higher section of this hill). Between the quarries and the ruins previously mentioned, there is an empty space about 200 m long.

Coming up from the valley, on the northwestern side, a steep path leads through a sort of cutting, or "gate," 2.5 to 3 m high and 3 to 4 m wide.

There are several tombs cut in the rock. There are also many cisterns or silos.

On the south-southeast side of the northeastern hill, and a few hundred yards from it, there is a large reservoir on the bottom of the valley. It is 30 m long and 20 m wide, similar in size to the "pools of Solomon." It is cased with stones of good masonry. There are also remains of watercourses in the same vicinity.

On the ruins, pottery identified as coming from the Middle Bronze Age, through the Late Bronze Age, Early Iron I, Nabatean, Roman, and medieval Arabic times has been picked up. Some coins have also been found.

References

Anderson, B. W.
1964 *ASOR Newsletter,* No. 3 (Jan. 4).

Conder, C. R.
1882 Lieutenant Conder's Report No. IX: Heshbon and Its Cromlechs. *PEFQS* 14: 7-15.

1892 *Heth and Moab.* London: Alexander P. Watt.

Garstang, J.
1931 *The Foundations of Bible History: Joshua, Judges.* London: Constable.

Glueck, N.
1934 Explorations in Eastern Palestine, I. *Annual of the American Schools of Oriental Research* 14: 1-113.

Heidet, L.
1903 Hésébon. Cols. 657-663 in vol. 3 of *Dictionnaire de la Bible,* ed. F. G. Vigouroux. Paris: Letouzey et Ané.

James, E. G.
1954 Hesbon. Pp. 1062-1063 in vol. 1 of *Dictionary of Greek and Roman Geography,* ed. W. Smith. Boston: Little, Brown.

McClintock, J., and Strong, J., eds.
1894 Heshbon. P. 220 in vol. 4 of *Cyclopaedia of Biblical, Theological, and Ecclesiastical Literature.* New York: Harper.

Post, G. A.
1888 Narrative of a Scientific Expedition in the Trans-Jordanic Region in the Spring of 1886. *PEFQS* 20: 175-237.

Robinson, E.
1841 *Biblical Researches in Palestine, Mount Sinai and Arabia Petraea,* vol. 2. Boston: Crocker and Brewster.

Saller, S. J. and Bagatti, B.
1949 *The Town of Nebo.* Jerusalem: Franciscan.

Saulcy, F. de
1865 *Voyage en Terre Sainte,* vol. I. Paris: Didier.

Seetzen, J. J.
1854 *Reisen duch Syrien, Palästina, Phönicien, die Transjordan-Länder, Arabia Petraea und Unter-Aegypten,* vol. 1. Berlin: Reimer.

Sejourné, P.-M.
1893 Chronique. *RB* 2: 119-145.

Simons, J.
1959 *The Geographical and Topographical Texts of the Old Testament.* Leiden: Brill.

Thomson, W. M.
1885 *The Land and the Book.* New York: Harper.

Tobler, T.
1867 *Bibliographia Geographica Palaestinae.* Leipzig: Hirzel.

Tristram, H. B.
1865 *The Land of Israel: A Journal of Travels in Palestine.* London: Society for Promoting Christian Knowledge.

Endnotes

[1] J. S. Buckingham, *Travels in Palestine Through the Countries of Bashan and Gilead, East of the River Jordan: Including a Visit to the Countries of Geraza and Gamala* (London: Longman, 1821). The information on the title is given by Tobler (1867: 143). The quotation is taken from McClintock and Strong (1894: 220).

[2] C. L. Irby and J. Mangles, *Travels,* p. 472, as quoted by McClintock and Strong (1894: 220). Tobler (1867: 145) gives the title of the book as *Travels Through Nubia, Palestine and Syria in 1816 and 1817.*

[3] The title of Porter's book is given by Tobler as *A Handbook for Travellers in Syria and Palestine* (London: J. Murray, 1858).

[4] Porter (1858: 298), as referred to by McClintock and Strong (1894: 220).

[5] The phrase, in French, is: ". . . est un soubassement d'édicule." *Édicule* is also translated as: miniature temple or church; public convenience, etc.

[6] James (1854: 1063) writes: "Near the tent village of Hûsban are the ruins of ancient Hesbon." What does he mean by "tent village"? It was probably a temporary Bedouin camp, seen and reported by a traveller.

[7] The modern road runs east of the ruins.

[8] The LXX reads: 'οφθαλμοι σου ως λιμναι εν ΕσεΒων εν πυλαις θυγατχος πολλων. The Vulgate reads: Oculi tui sicut piscinae in Hesebon, Quae sunt in porta filiae multitudinis."

[9] Saller and Bagatti base their statement on Musil's *Arabia Petraea: I. Moab* (Wien, 1907), p. 388, and fig. 180 NW.

[10] On p. 75 Glueck mentions that one piece (No. 26 in pl. 27) of a "fine rouletted Nabatean" sherd came from Hesban. He also ascribes (p. 76) to the Nabatean Period a fragment of sigillata ware found there (pl. 26b), and another piece of rouletted sigillata (pl. 28).

AUTHOR INDEX

Author Index

BIBLICAL REFERENCE INDEX

Biblical Reference Index

GENERAL INDEX

General Index